HELEN Preckel.

HELEN Preckel.

THE MARGARET BOYLES BOOK OF NEEDLE ART

ALSO BY MARGARET BOYLES:

NEEDLEPOINT STITCHERY
BARGELLO: AN EXPLOSION IN COLOR
AMERICAN INDIAN NEEDLEPOINT
WORKBOOK
THE MARGARET BOYLES BARGELLO
WORKBOOK
NEEDLEWORK CALENDAR, 1977

THE MARGARET BOYLES BOOK OF
NEEDLE ART

HARCOURT BRACE JOVANOVICH
NEW YORK AND LONDON

FOR MY BELOVED NANCY BLAINE

DESIGN: ULRICH RUCHTI

COPYRIGHT © 1978 BY MARGARET BOYLES

Printed in the United States of America

Library of Congress Cataloging in Publication Data
Boyles, Margaret.
    Margaret Boyles Book of needle art.

    Includes index.
    1. Embroidery. I. Title. II. Title: Book of
needle art.
TT770.B69 1978   746.4′4   77–73064
ISBN 0–15–157100–7
ISBN 0-15-657964-2 (paperback)

First edition

B C D E

CONTENTS

INTRODUCTION

A long time ago a little girl finished her embroidered sampler with the words "Patty Polk did this and she hated every stitch she did in it." I have just finished *my* sampler—this book—and unlike Patty, I loved every minute spent on the embroideries in it. I hope it will bring as much pleasure and joy to all of you.

A love of good needlework is contagious, and I have been privileged in the last few years to share my enthusiasm and delight with many. The potpourri of projects within this book is a very personal blend of the things I like and hope will appeal to my readers. Many of them are from my home—my desk chair, a wing chair from the living room, pastel pillows and a sampler from a bedroom, my scissors case, my grandson's birth certificate that was adapted from a Pennsylvania Dutch Taufschein. These demonstrate the double pleasure to be reaped from good needlework. It is a happy, relaxing pastime that produces things that are a joy to use for many years.

Included in the sampling of embroideries are traditional and Four-way Bargello, needlepoint, crewelpoint, crewel, Cross Stitch, and Florentine Embroidery. There are complete instructions for each project and lots of photographs and full-color charts to make sure no one will be tempted to finish with Patty's inscription. A list of materials with each assures exact duplication of the finished projects shown, makes shopping easy, and leaves all the pleasure to you. Enjoy every stitch! Have fun!

Margaret Boyles

EMBROIDERY ON CANVAS

EMBROIDERY ON CANVAS

Simply defined, *embroidery* is the use of stitches for the purpose of ornamentation or decoration. That broad interpretation includes many categories of the needle arts, and thus this book, conceived as a sampler, contains small "samples" of a variety of embroideries. Using the foundation material as the criteria for establishing a differentiation, these "samples" have been divided into the two general classifications of *Embroidery on Canvas* and *Embroidery on Fabric*. This is actually the clearest distinction that can be established, since the same stitches are used interchangeably on either foundation and many working techniques apply to both.

This section, covering Embroidery on Canvas, includes basic needlepoint, crewelpoint, Bargello, and Florentine Embroidery. The range of projects runs the gamut in size from a small eyeglasses case to a wing chair upholstered in Florentine Embroidery.

Each project is shown in full color, and many have additional detail photographs that are valuable working aids. For each project there is also a chart in the same colors as the finished model, a list of the materials needed, and complete working instructions. If these are followed accurately, it is possible to duplicate the finished article exactly. Stitch and finishing instructions follow the Embroidery on Fabric section. Use these guides to their fullest. They have been written to insure success with every venture.

MATERIALS

Yarns

The list of materials for each project contains all the information necessary to make shopping easy and to make duplication of the finished articles possible. Canvas requirements include allowances for unworked borders. The best-size needle is noted. The yarns and the manufacturer's color numbers are listed. These numbers are for either Columbia-Minerva Needlepoint and Crewel Yarn or Paternayan Persian Yarn. The numbers followed by an asterisk (*) can be found only in the Paternayan. The two brands can be mixed freely as both are three-ply wool Persian-type yarn and have the same color standards. When the yarn requirements are stated in skeins, the number is based on a 25-yard skein. Of course, other brands of yarn can be used if the colors are available, but be careful to check yardage as it varies from brand to brand.

The yarn requirements stated for each project are based on the amount of yarn used to complete the finished model. The quantity should be adequate for the average careful worker to finish the piece with a small surplus. The working methods used to determine the estimates were normal ones, with no special emphasis on conservation of yarn, but no material was wasted. If you know you are extravagant with yarn, or decide either to change the stitches or to enlarge the article, please buy additional yarn to compensate for the changes.

Whenever possible, buy all the yarn for a given project at the same time. Many yarns carry a dye lot number, and there is a very slight difference in the colors from lot to lot. The frustration caused by running out of yarn in a specific dye lot and the hassle of trying to find it or a close-enough match are things we can all do without. Buy enough or a little extra and relax. Leftovers are always handy for spur-of-the-moment projects, and unopened skeins can usually be returned or exchanged.

Persian yarns are wool and sufficiently long-wearing for most projects. They are available in a wide range of colors to suit any need. Because they are three-ply with a slight twist they can be used on various sizes of canvas by separating the plies and using as much as needed. Each project notes the number of plies that should be used for the canvas recommended for that particular piece.

The technicalities of dyeing wool cause very slight variations in the weight of the yarn from color to color. In many cases all the light colors are fine, but the dark ones are just slightly thinner. If, for this reason or any other, the recommended yarn does not cover the canvas properly, try stitching those colors with a slightly looser tension. If that does not solve the problem, separate the strands to remove the twist. If coverage is still lacking, give the yarn a steam bath by placing it in a steamer over boiling water for two or three minutes. If all else fails, add an additional ply to those being used, but remember to purchase a little more as this will use up yarn more quickly than was planned.

Change colors freely to customize the designs for your own needs. In many cases I have suggested these alterations as this is one of the biggest advantages of working from a book. Enjoy all the possibilities!

Canvas

A variety of canvas weaves and mesh counts have been used in the construction of the projects in this section. The list of materials identifies the mesh size, weave, and color of the canvas for each project. If exact duplication of the finished prod-

uct is desired, the canvas should meet the specifications noted. A change to larger or smaller mesh will alter the size of the article and invalidate the yarn requirement list.

Charts

The color charts for the Bargello and Florentine designs are probably the clearest ever devised, recreating as they do the embroidery itself in graphic detail. To use these charts, count the squares within the colored outline which represents a stitch and make a stitch on the canvas over the corresponding number of threads. (Count canvas threads, not holes.) Color placement is indicated on the charts by hues as close as possible to those of the yarn, except when the colors are so closely graded that true duplication would make differentiation of rows difficult. In these cases the shades have been slightly modified to separate the rows distinctly. Colors are always keyed to the yarn numbers immediately below the chart to avoid confusion. Following the chart is further simplified by cues in the body of instructions as to the best working method for each piece.

Other needlepoint charts in this section include full-color graphs for counted design and outline drawings to be traced onto the canvas. Instructions for the use of these charts appear with illustrations of the finished articles made from them.

Frames, Thimble, Scissors, and Needles

The use of a frame in working canvas embroidery is optional. With a frame the work is naturally less portable and there is a slight adjustment in working methods, but the canvas maintains its shape and remains crisp and new. Beautiful stitches are possible either way, so the decision about using a frame should be based purely on personal preference.

Good embroidery scissors are a must and they should be reserved for embroidery only. Keep them in a case to protect them as well as the needlepoint.

Beautiful embroidery can be worked with or without a thimble. Many cannot work without one, while others find the thimble clumsy and awkward. Therefore, the decision to use one or not is again purely personal.

Keep an assortment of various sizes of Tapestry needles to make sure the right one is on hand when a new project is started. The best size for each piece is included in the materials list, but keep in mind that, again, individual preferences may indicate using a smaller or larger size.

PREPARING THE CANVAS

Canvas Borders

When a project is planned, a 2-inch border of unworked canvas should be allowed on all sides of the piece. This is not a waste of canvas but an essential and functional border that helps maintain the canvas shape and makes blocking possible (see the Finishing section). Small projects may require a smaller border, but most need the full 2 inches. The estimates for canvas requirements for individual projects include allowance for this border.

Taping the Canvas

Tape the cut edges of the canvas with masking tape to prevent fraying and to keep the yarn from snagging on the stiff threads as the embroidery is being worked. Use only masking tape; other tapes work loose and sometimes leave a sticky deposit on the canvas.

Marking Pens

Exercise care in choosing marking pens that are to be used on canvas. Many new ones are made especially for use on canvas; others intended for general use are also waterproof when dry and are safe for needlepoint. To be safe, always test a marker before using it, regardless of what the label says.

Avoid using markers in black or other dark colors, for they tend to show through light-colored yarn. Pink, pale blue, orange, grey, and light green are good choices. The lines need only be dark enough to be visible.

Dividing the Canvas

It is very important that needlepoint and Bargello designs be centered, and in most cases this is quickly done by drawing a series of lines on the canvas before the work is started. Chart #1 represents a needlepoint canvas marked with the lines needed for most projects.

Lines *A* and *B* on the chart cross at the center of the canvas and divide it into four equal segments. These two lines are necessary for all Bargello and are also often used for centering line drawings and counted designs.

Diagonal Lines *C* and *D*, which also intersect at the center of the canvas, are the miter lines needed in addition to Lines *A* and *B* for Four-way Bargello.

Some designs need only Lines *A* and *B*. Others need all four. The instructions for each project state which lines are going to be needed. In addition, the lines are shown on the charts for the projects as dashed lines and are marked *A* and *B* to help orient the chart to the canvas.

To mark the canvas, fold it into quarters and mark the center mesh (*x* on

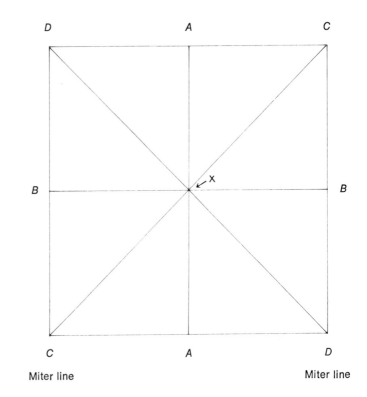

D · A · C

B · B

C · A · D

Miter line · Miter line

Preparing the Canvas

CHART #1.

This diagram represents a canvas with the four guidelines used for Bargello and Four-way Bargello, and for centering line drawings and counted designs. Lines *A* and *B*, dividing the canvas into four quarters, are needed for any Bargello project and as a guide to centering any other type of design. Lines *C* and *D* are the miter lines necessary for Four-way Bargello. Some designs need only the first two lines, others need all four. The diagram and instructions for each project indicate which lines are necessary for its completion.

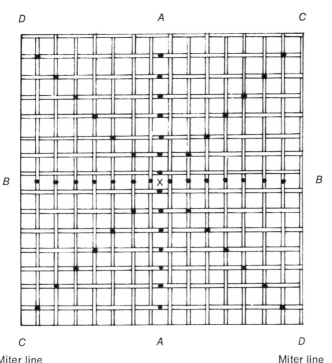

D · A · C

B · B

C · A · D

Miter line · Miter line

CHART #2.

This enlarged detail of the center portion of a marked canvas shows the dividing lines as dots as they will appear on the canvas. Note the way lines *C* and *D* move out from the center mesh (*x*) on the true diagonal. It is of great importance that these lines be drawn accurately.

13

the charts). Open the canvas flat and draw Lines *A* and *B* so they intersect in the center mesh. Draw the lines between two threads so they appear as dots on the cross-threads as on Chart #2.

The two diagonal miter lines, when needed, must be drawn carefully, thread by thread, to insure accurate placement. Do not attempt to use a straightedge for this task. Although it sounds painstaking, it takes only a few minutes to place the lines. Begin at the corners of the center mesh and move diagonally outward, placing a dot on the threads as shown in Chart #2. The dots need only be dark enough to be a guide.

WORKING TECHNIQUES

Needlepoint is not a difficult or complicated embroidery, but good working habits and methods are important and are evident in the finished product. Work patiently, enjoying the process of making the stitches and striving to make each stitch perfect. Take your time!

Use only high-quality materials. It is false economy to choose cheap canvas or yarn—not only do they not last, they are much more difficult to use. One experience with poor materials can be enough to discourage a beginner from ever trying needlepoint again. Then, too, there is the purely practical angle—a chair seat upholstered in Bargello or needlepoint made of high-quality materials may never need recovering, while one of lesser quality will become shabby in a short time.

Care of Canvas

During the working period, take care of canvas that is not being worked on a frame. Keep it clean and protected by rolling it in a towel before tucking it into the work basket or bag. Avoid folding and refolding it along the same mesh, as this eventually destroys the sizing in the fold and loosens the threads, making it difficult to work smooth, even stitches in that row. Also protect the canvas from damage from the embroidery scissors by keeping them in a little case of their own.

Threading the Needle

Illustrated on the facing page are two methods of threading a needle with yarn. Another correct but seldom mentioned method is to press the end of the yarn between the thumb and forefinger of the one hand and with the other hand force the eye of the needle over the yarn as it is held tightly. With only a little practice the yarn will slip right into the eye.

The paper method is foolproof— always successful even with yarn that tends to fray and split. Any of the three techniques is good. Never wet or twist yarn in order to get it through the eye of the needle.

Mistakes

Some experts advance a theory that a few mistakes add an element of charm to embroidery, but this is very often used as an excuse for carelessness. Moreover, it is simply not true. A mistake does not add one positive element to an embroidery, but it will definitely detract from the embroiderer's enjoyment of the finished piece, as it will always be the first thing she sees when she looks at it. A good design well executed is a tribute to the embroiderer's skill, and it should not be marred with a mistake. Rip out the stitches and correct them as soon as the error is discovered.

Waste Knot

The only knot ever used for canvas embroidery is the Waste Knot, which is re-

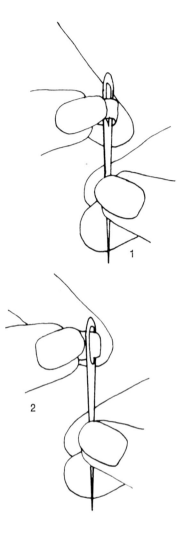

FOLD METHOD (left)
1. Hold the needle between the thumb and forefinger with the eye facing you. Fold the yarn across the eye of the needle and pull tightly to form a sharp fold.
2. Force the fold through the eye of the needle.

PAPER METHOD (above)
1. Cut a small piece of paper about an inch long and narrow enough to fit through the eye of the needle. Fold the paper as shown in the drawing and place the cut end of the yarn into the fold.
2. Pass the folded end of the paper through the eye of the needle and the yarn will be carried through quite easily.

moved after it has served its purpose. (See illustration, page 16.) The knot is placed on the right side of the canvas several inches from the area to be embroidered. The stitches are worked through the long strand on the back until it is fastened. The knot is then cut off and all traces of its having been used are gone.

A knot of any type left in the canvas embroidery will make a raised spot on the surface, making it impossible to achieve the smooth, even surface needed for good appearance.

Beginning and Ending
Attach the yarn for the first few stitches either with a Waste Knot or by holding

the end of yarn on the back and working through it until it is fastened. Begin subsequent strands by pulling them through the back of the last four or five stitches worked.

End a strand of yarn by pulling it through the back of four or five stitches in the row above. Never begin and end in the same group of stitches, as this pulls the stitches tightly on the right side and causes a ridge that will not block out.

Clip the ends of yarn short to avoid tangling and to keep them from being pulled to the right side as new stitches are worked. This is particularly important when a large number of colors is being used.

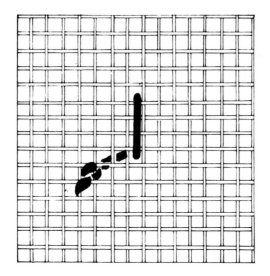

The Waste Knot is placed on the right side of the canvas about 2″ from the starting point. (*Note:* Illustration is not to scale.) The first stitches are worked through the long strand on the back, fastening it. The knot is then cut off, and all evidence that it was used disappears.

Yarn Twisting and Wearing Thin

If the yarn becomes twisted as you work —a natural occurrence—hold the canvas up, drop the needle, and let the yarn unwind itself. Do not continue to work with the twisted yarn; it will not cover the canvas well, and the stitches will have a slightly different shape due to the twist.

It is possible to prevent the yarn from twisting while working. As the needle is drawn out of the canvas at the completion of a stitch, roll it about a quarter-turn in the direction of the canvas. A little pressure from the thumb is all that it takes to do this, and it quickly becomes an automatic gesture. It may seem too simple to work, but it does!

CREWELPOINT

The term *crewelpoint* is a recently coined one used to describe a canvas embroidery which is needlepoint embellished with stitches usually associated with crewelwork. The use of the free or surface stitches on the canvas makes it possible to achieve shapes and textures not obtainable with needlepoint alone. This combination of techniques is very satisfying and is a great deal of fun.

When using crewel or surface embroidery stitches on canvas, work without regard to the canvas threads just as if the stitches were being worked on fabric. The stitches may be worked on top of Tent Stitch or can be placed directly on the canvas. Usually better canvas coverage results if the Tent Stitch area adjoining the surface stitches is worked first so the free stitches can overlap the edge of the flatter Tent Stitches. If the surface stitches are worked directly on the canvas, they should be placed close together so no canvas is visible between them. French

Knots should be clustered; rows of stitches should lie against each other; Turkey work should be done in small stitches in closely spaced rows; and Satin Stitch should be padded with stitches lying in the opposite direction to the surface stitches, and the surface stitches themselves should be close together.

BARGELLO

Count the Bargello stitches carefully, following the given chart until the pattern is established. Accuracy is essential, for very often a line or lines delineate a pattern and all other rows merely follow. If a mistake is made in the first row, it will carry into all subsequent rows. Do not waste time trying to work around an error. It seems that the more effort one puts into trying to work around a mistake, the worse it becomes.

Since Bargello stitches are long, they use up yarn quickly, and so it is possible to work with a strand longer than is generally used for other needlepoint stitches. A length of 15 to 18 inches is usually comfortable. Greater lengths are more awkward to handle, and the yarn might wear thin.

Learn to work the Bargello stitches with a light, even tension. The stitches lie upright on the canvas and must be loose enough to allow the yarn to "fluff out" and cover the canvas. If the canvas threads are visible between the stitches, either the stitches are too tight or the yarn is not heavy enough to cover the canvas being used. Try stitching with a lighter tension. If that does not solve the problem, try one of the methods of increasing the bulk of the yarn described on page 11.

Bargello stitches should lie flat on the canvas with no twisting of the yarn on the right side of the embroidery. Take time to guide the yarn into a perfect stitch every time. The smooth, even surface that results enhances the beauty of the Bargello designs.

Many Bargello designs depend heavily upon delicate shadings of color that are difficult to differentiate under artificial light. To avoid making mistakes, sort and mark colors in daylight.

In many of the Bargello projects here, rows of Upright Gobelin Stitch are used for border details. To turn the corner of a Gobelin border row neatly, work as shown on the chart on page 18, placing a diagonal stitch over the line where the stitches meet. The stitches in the chart are worked over 4 threads, but the principle applies to stitches of any length. The finished look is both neat and attractive.

Rows of Gobelin Stitch tend to have rows of tiny canvas specks showing between them no matter how carefully the stitches have been worked. The problem is inherent in the upright stitches, but to the perfectionist it is very annoying. A row of Back Stitch worked with a single strand of yarn in matching color between the rows covers the exposed threads very effectively. At the same time the little Back Stitches make the Gobelin rows seem to be raised a little above the rest of the embroidery—a very nice look.

FOUR-WAY BARGELLO

Four-way or Mitered Bargello is one of the most exciting and challenging forms of canvas embroidery. When the canvas is divided into four triangles and the design worked out from the center in four directions, the simplest of Bargello lines make intriguing patterns. Working the mitered design requires more skill and

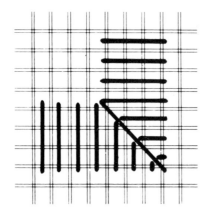

To make a neat corner for a Gobelin border, decrease the length of stitches as shown, turn the canvas, and gradually increase until the full length of stitches is again reached. Place a diagonal stitch over the line where the stitches join to make a neat finish. The stitches shown are drawn over 4 threads, but the principle holds for stitches of any length.

thought than the average Bargello, but once the mechanics have been mastered they are within the scope of most needleworkers.

When possible it is best to begin working a Four-way design at the center of the canvas, progressing outward while keeping the design within the confines of the miter lines. It is necessary to make adjustments in the length of some of the stitches along the miter lines to form a neat line. The charts for these projects show these adjustments in detail. In many cases when a stitch of the length used in the design would leave a single thread along the miter, a longer stitch has been substituted. This avoids making a stitch over a single thread that usually will not lie flat. Occasionally, however, when it is important that a color be carried up to a sharp point, the neat stitch is sacrificed for better color placement.

Although it is usually best to begin a Four-way design in the center of the canvas, there is absolutely no definite order in which the balance of a piece must be worked. Whichever method produces the best Bargello with the least effort is best, and this can vary from person to person as well as from design to design. While one person may prefer to work each section completely before beginning the next, another might embroider the center portions of all four triangles and work outward on all four quadrants at the same time. The instructions suggest the best working order for each specific piece, but these can be freely changed at the reader's preference.

THE FLORENTINE COLLECTION

THE FLORENTINE COLLECTION

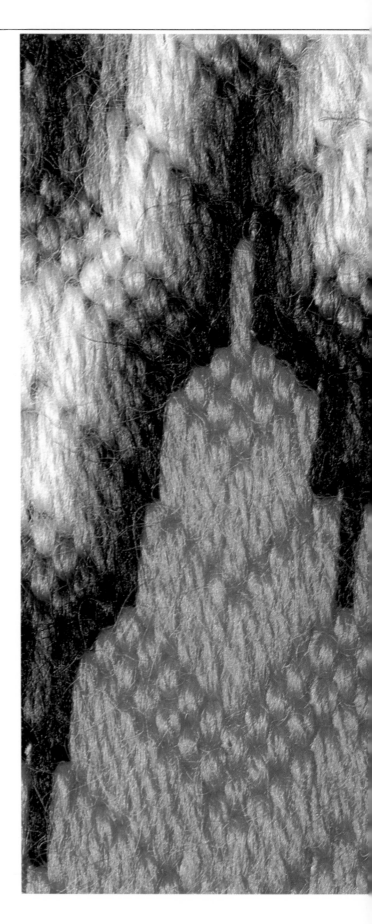

The romance of Bargello includes the story of a Hungarian princess who brought to Florence in her dowry trunks exquisite examples of Point de Hongrie, a counted embroidery new to her adopted country. The princess is said to have taught her ladies-in-waiting to copy the lovely designs, and the work became so popular in the area that it is still called Florentine Embroidery.

Although there is little to substantiate the legend, the story does enrich the intriguing history of embroidery, and it is fun to speculate about the origins of a stitch or design as our modern needles trace the treasured designs onto canvas.

Florentine Embroidery is a special kind of Bargello. Like Bargello it is worked in the Upright Gobelin Stitch. One characteristic that distinguishes Florentine is the use of a combination of long and short stitches to produce a secondary stitching pattern in addition to the pattern of the color design. Another striking feature is the distinctive appearance that is derived from the combination of stitch lengths. A Florentine Flame has an interesting "extra" when compared to a flame design worked in a traditional Bargello 4-2 or 4-1 step.

The secondary pattern that develops as a result of a stitching repeat that always places two long stitches over two short ones is readily apparent in the plain pink section of this detail from a large piece. The design is similar to the one used for the Pencil Holder on pages 28–29, but with broad black and grey stripes on the pink background.

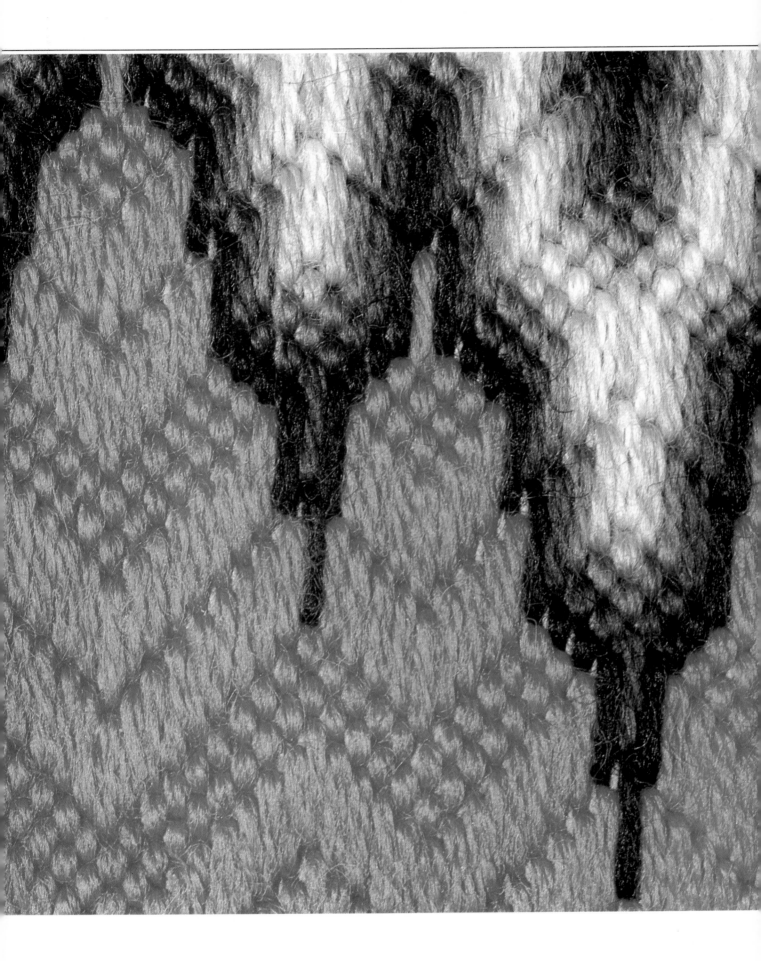

THE FLORENTINE COLLECTION

Florentine designs are many and varied. Perhaps best known is the one appearing on a famous set of seventeenth-century armchairs in the Museo Nazionale in Florence, Italy (known locally as "the Bargello Museum"). The lovely pattern is worked in silk in soft shades of yellow, white, green, and deep blue. It has been photographed and copied extensively in the past few years.

Many of the surviving examples of old Florentine work are bed hangings, curtains, altar pieces, and other large articles. Flame patterns worked in a myriad of colors were often used on these pieces, and because of the size of the pieces the Flame line often meandered from one side to the other, with little attention to a regular repeat or to centering the design. Colors were sometimes well used and carefully planned, but at other times their use was erratic, and it often appears that when the supply of one was exhausted another was substituted and the work continued. There is great charm in these early pieces, and one must admire the tenacity needed to complete such ambitious projects. Imagine the time involved in embroidering a set of hangings and a spread for one of those massive four-posters of long ago!

Florentine work for use today is every bit as lovely as the old pieces and is a most satisfying and interesting kind of Bargello. At first consideration, the combination of stitch lengths may appear confusing and an unnecessary complication, but observation of the details of the embroidery prove otherwise. The stitching pattern is entirely logical and the results gratifying. There is a key to each pattern than can be found by "reading" up or down a single row of mesh. The stitches are always in regular sequence. It may be two long stitches alternating with two short ones, one long stitch followed by a short one and repeating, or perhaps one long stitch succeeding two short ones. Whichever pattern, it will always be regular throughout the piece.

Given a chart for the first row, a listed color sequence, and the key to the stitching pattern, most people can duplicate a design with no problems. Any question as to which size stitch to make next is answered by the stitches directly above the stitch in question. The simple logic of it prevents confusion. The following lesson is designed as a first experiment with this work and will banish any doubts about even a beginner's ability to create these designs. If you have never experimented with them, practice a few rows using the charts and notes.

Above right: Lovely colonial American colors highlight an easy Florentine pattern worked in long stitches over 6 threads and short ones over 2 threads. The stitch pattern for this piece is an interesting variation which places one long stitch over a short one. Right: This detail of a section of the Wishbone design shows a stitch pattern that places one long stitch over two short ones to create a lovely old Florentine favorite. The use of contrasting colors makes the piece bright, while the placement of the colors accents the horizontal pattern rows.

A LESSON IN FLORENTINE EMBROIDERY

Work on #10 white mono canvas with three- or four-ply Persian wool so the stitches will be large and easy to see. Use bright colors to match the charts so that rows are distinct and are oriented color-wise to the charts.

This practice piece is not intended for any use other than gaining an understanding of the way the stitches are placed on the canvas. The charted design is merely a line showing one-and-a-half peaks of a Flame design, which is enough to illustrate the changes in stitching pattern at both the inside and outside of the peaks. Each square on the chart represents 1 thread on the canvas. The long stitches are worked over 6 threads, the short ones over 2.

As the row is worked upward toward the peak of the Flame, the bottom of each new stitch is 1 thread below the top of the previous stitch, creating the steep slope. As the row is worked downward on the other side of the slope, the top of each new stitch is 1 thread above the bottom of the last stitch.

The chart for Row 1 shows the line of stitching in red. On the next diagram, Row 2 is shown in yellow and is placed directly under the red row as it will appear on your canvas. Similarly, the charts for Rows 3 and 4 show the new rows added to the already-completed ones on the canvas. Row 3 is shown in blue, Row 4 in green.

ROW 1. Beginning at the right side of the canvas at least 45 mesh from the top, so there is room for the peak, work Row 1 to Stitch C, placing the stitches as charted. Check to determine that Stitches A and C line up on the same horizontal thread of the canvas. If they do not, there is probably an error in counting, and this is the best time to find and correct it. Continue working the row to Stitch D at the top and check again to make certain that Stitches B and D also line up on a single horizontal thread. It is a good idea to form the habit of automatically checking points like this to insure accuracy and avoid making counting errors that must be corrected later.

ROW 2. With yellow yarn begin Row 2 with a small stitch. Finish the row following the chart and noting the way in which the long and short stitches alternate.

ROW 3. Row 3 is blue and begins with a small stitch directly under the short yellow stitch at the start of Row 2. Note that the second stitches of Rows 1 and 2 were both long. In order to maintain the stitching rhythm of placing two short stitches under two long ones, it is therefore necessary to make the second stitch of Row 3 a short one. Continue working the row, paying particular attention to the way the stitch pattern is emerging.

ROW 4. Row 4, which is green, begins with a long stitch, since the two directly above it are short. The rhythm is now becoming obvious and you can probably work the balance of the row without benefit of the chart. Try it!

Some of the following projects include complete row-by-row charts for the entire piece in order to provide a reference for those insecure about the Florentine stitching patterns, but once the rhythm is understood it is usually much easier to work from a diagram of the first row only. If you are a beginner, try first the fully charted design and then progress to the single-row charts (such as the Blue-Rust Florentine Pillow).

24

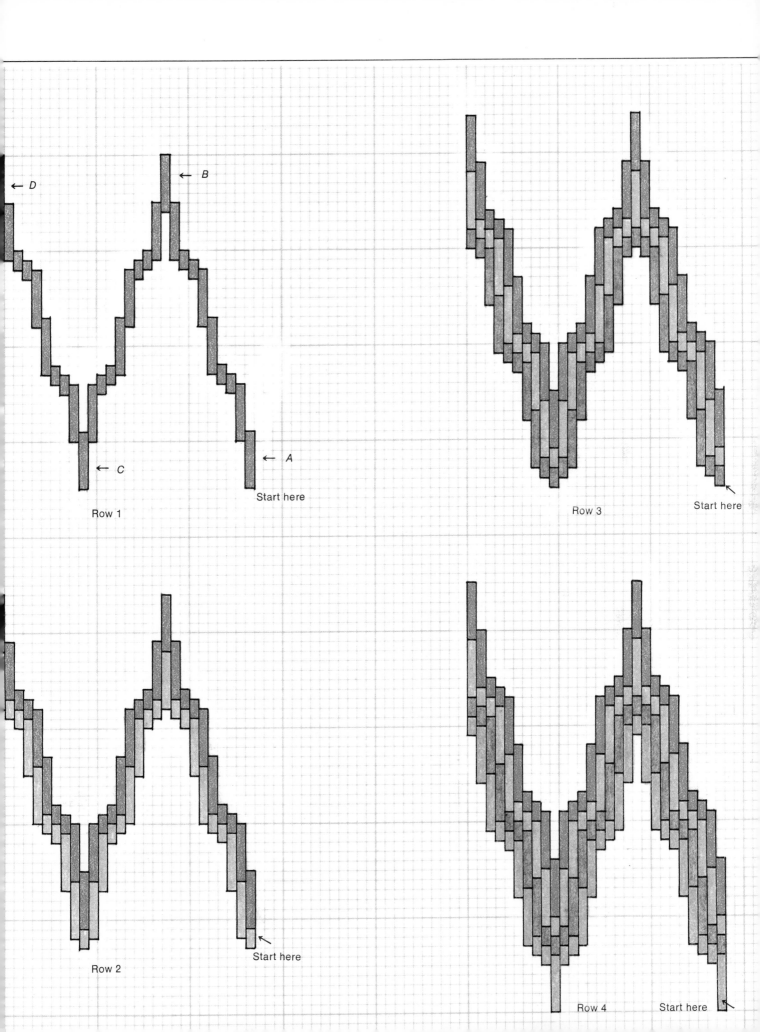

← D

← B

← C

← A

Start here

Row 1

Start here

Row 3

Start here

Row 2

Row 4   Start here

FLORENTINE EYEGLASSES CASE

Pale neutral shades of beige combine in the Florentine Flame pattern to make a pretty glasses case. This is an ideal first venture into these interesting stitching techniques. The chart shows every row of the case as a reference and aid to those who may become confused by the changes in stitch length. Actually, it is not *all* that complicated—I think you will agree when you have finished the glasses case.

Finished size: 3" × 6"
Materials: #14 white mono canvas
    10" × 10"
#20 tapestry needle
Persian yarn, 1 skein of each: 136–Sand;
    492–Dust; 020–Neutral; 012–Ivory
Fabric for lining: approximately 7" × 7"
Note: Separate the yarn and work with
    two-ply throughout.

Instructions: Tape the canvas. Begin Row 1 at top right with Sand (136), placing Stitch *a* 2" in from side edge and 4" down from the top of the canvas. Following the chart, carefully count the row from *a* to *b*. Repeat the line "in reverse"—that is, *read the chart* from *c* to *a*, but *work on the canvas* in the direction of the heavy arrow—to complete the front half of the case. Continuing across the canvas, repeat the process for the back section.

Work downward, shading the colors from dark to light and repeating as shown on the chart. Keep the chart handy for reference, but you will soon find you do not need it if you always remember to work two short stitches under two long ones.

When 16 full rows have been worked, fill in the unfinished spaces at the edge with partial rows to form a straight edge. Maintain the color sequence to the bottom of the case.

At the top of the case fill in the unworked spaces entirely with Sand (136), maintaining the stitching pattern as established. Work one row of Upright Gobelin Stitch along top edge to form a border. With a single strand of matching yarn work a row of Back Stitches between the Gobelin row and the Florentine rows.

Block and construct case.

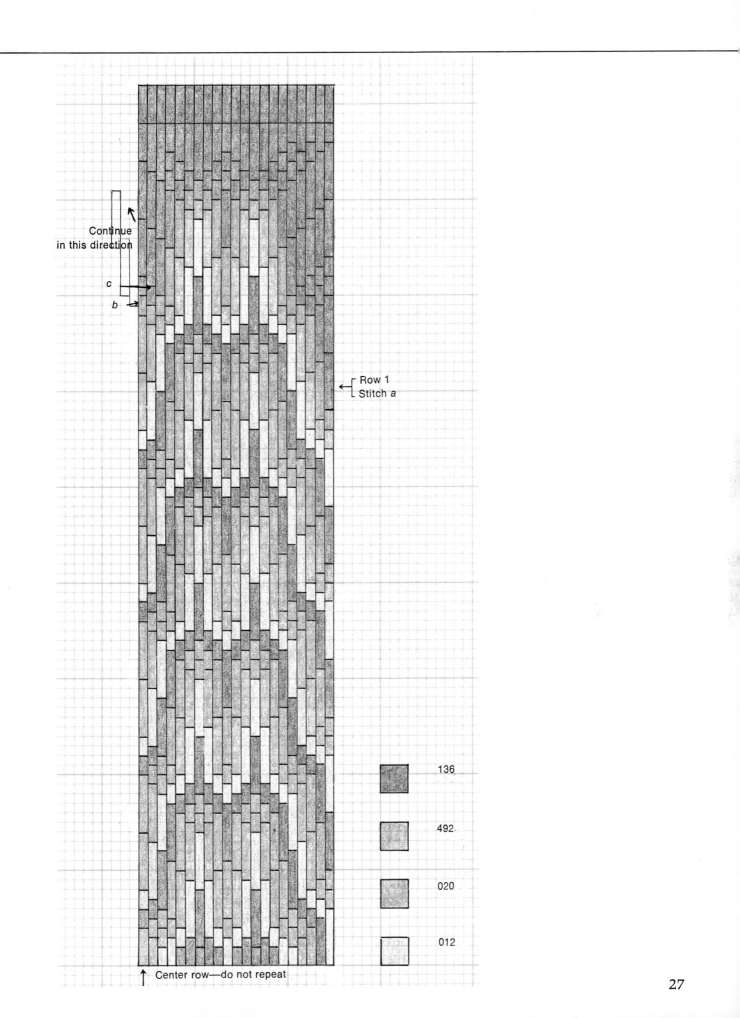

Continue
in this direction

c

b

Row 1
Stitch *a*

136

492

020

012

Center row—do not repeat

PENCIL HOLDER

Bargello and a coat of spray paint transform a frozen juice container into an interesting desk accessory. The Bargello is a slight variation of the Florentine Flame seen on the pillow and chair on pages 34–37 and 42–44. This time it is worked in just three shades of rust. The piece of Bargello is small requiring only one repeat of the flame. Working the triangles of solid color between the points accents the steep peaks of the Flame and brings out the secondary pattern of the short stitches.

Finished size: 3½″ × 6½″
Materials: #14 white mono canvas
      10½″ × 6½″
#20 tapestry needle
Persian yarn, 1 skein of each: 414–Rust;
      416–Light Rust; 423–Pale Rust
An empty, clean 6-oz frozen juice can
Spray paint in complimentary color
Note: Separate the yarn and work with
      two-ply throughout.

Instructions: Begin working Row 1 at a point 1½″ in from both bottom and side edges of canvas at lower right corner. Work row from *a* to *b*, placing stitches as shown and alternating the lengths as indicated by the chart. Continue across the row, repeating the peak from *c* to *b* five more times to complete Row 1.

Work remaining 6 rows of the flame pattern following the chart for stitch placement and color sequence. As in most of the other Florentine designs in this group, two short stitches are always followed by two long ones when reading up or down rows.

Fill in the triangular spaces at edges with solid rust, following the stitching pattern established by the flame rows.

Block. Trim canvas edges to ½″. Press canvas allowances on the two long sides and one end to wrong side.

Spray-paint the inside and the exposed metal rims of the juice container. Coat the outside of the can with an even layer of one of the thick white craft glues. Allow to stand until tacky. Smooth the Bargello into place and hold until the glue sets. Several rubber bands placed at intervals will hold the canvas tight against the can until the glue is thoroughly dry.

28

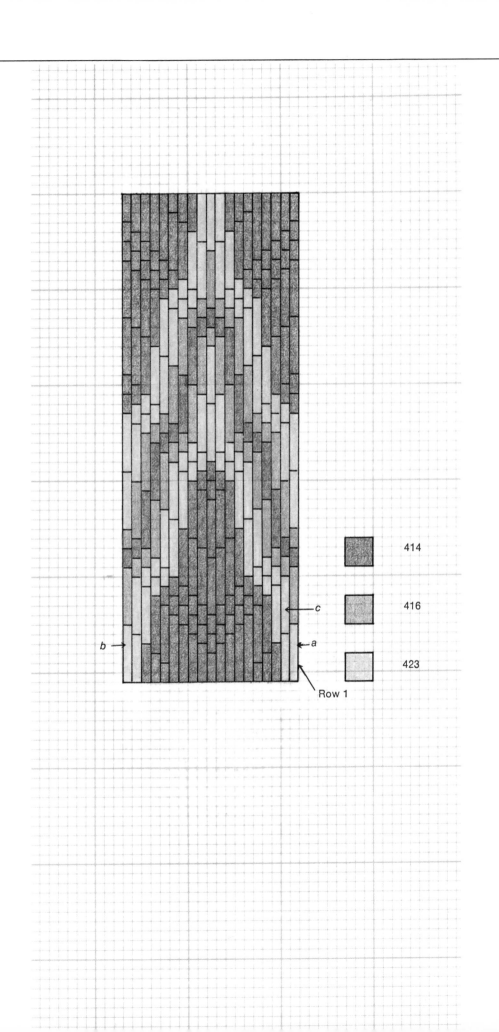

414

416

c

b →   ← *a*

423

Row 1

FLORENTINE SWAG PILLOW

This attractive little pillow is worked in one of the easier Florentine patterns—a version in which a stitch over 2 threads always follows a stitch over 6 threads when read up or down a row. The detail photograph and the chart show this graphically and make it clear that after the first row is counted correctly the subsequent rows follow easily.

Blues shading from navy through pale tones to white emphasize the swag effect of the inverted arches, while three-ply Persian yarn and #12 canvas make the work go quickly. Tassels are an interesting trim on oblong shapes such as this (see tassel-making instructions in the Finishing section at the end of the book).

Worked on #14 canvas, this adaptable design would be lovely as a chair seat or stool top. One repeat of the scallop is enough for an eyeglasses case, and when worked Four-way the design produces an intriguing kaleidoscopic effect. Coloring too can be widely varied—all monochromatic combinations are good; five soft Colonial colors or five pastels are charming.

Facing page: To be used as a construction aid, this closeup of a section of the pillow shows clearly the stitching pattern and color placement. The long stitches are worked over 6 threads, while the short ones are over 2. This is an easy pattern.

FLORENTINE SWAG PILLOW

Finished size: 9¾" × 11"
Materials: #12 white interlocking canvas
    14" × 15"
#20 tapestry needle
Persian yarn as follows: 334–Dark
    French Blue, 1 skein; 330–Old Blue,
    2 skeins; 756–Summer Blue, 2
    skeins; 395–Light Blue, 2 skeins;
    005–White, 1 skein
Fabric for pillow back: ½ yard
Note 1: Use yarn full-ply as it comes from
    the skein.
Note 2: If tassels are to be used (see Fin-
    ishing section), an extra skein of
    756–Summer Blue is needed.

Instructions: Tape the canvas and mark
Lines *A* and *B*. Begin working at center of
canvas with darkest color (334), placing
Stitch *a* on the vertical line (Line *A*) with
the bottom of the stitch touching the horizontal line (Line *B*). Count the row carefully to *b* and then repeat from *c* to *b* for
second scallop. End the yarn. Attach
again at center and work two repeats to
the left side. This completes the first row
and centers the design. All subsequent
rows can be worked in one sweep across
the canvas from right to left.

    The chart shows one complete color
repeat. Work downward using the shades
in the sequence shown. Row 9, which is
Dark French Blue (334), is the last full
row to the bottom edge of the piece. To
square the edge, fill in the remaining
arched sections working only the portions
of the rows needed.

    Turn the canvas and work 12 rows
in the established color sequence to fix the
top limit of the piece. Row 12, the last full
row, will be white. Complete the section
by working the portions of rows needed
to square the edge.

    Block and construct the pillow.

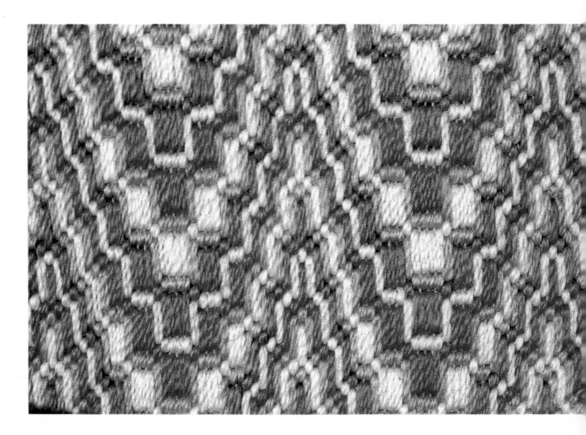

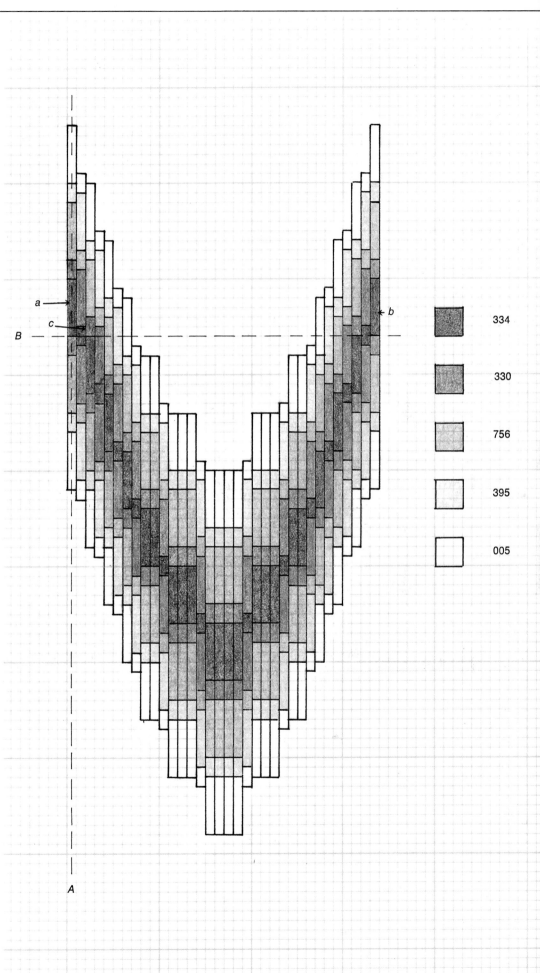

Facing page: This is the pillow design worked in a combination of Old Rose, French Blue, Ivory, and Soft Green. The multicolor scheme works up into a pillow with a bright, refreshing look.

334

330

756

395

005

BLUE-RUST FLORENTINE PILLOW

The wing chair pattern (pp. 42–43) worked in bold stripes of French blue and rust makes an interesting pillow to finish with plump tassels. Using the wide stripes of two colors creates a dramatic change in the appearance of the pattern. Many of the old versions of this pattern used color in this manner, while some included stripes of five or six colors. Some that were obviously planned to use leftover yarn utilized many colors, and if well done are a veritable rainbow of color and pattern.

Facing page: This view shows in detail the delicate color shading and the stitching pattern for the pillow. This is the design used also for the Gold Chair on pages 42–44. The detail photograph shown there illustrates the design worked in a monochromatic color scheme.

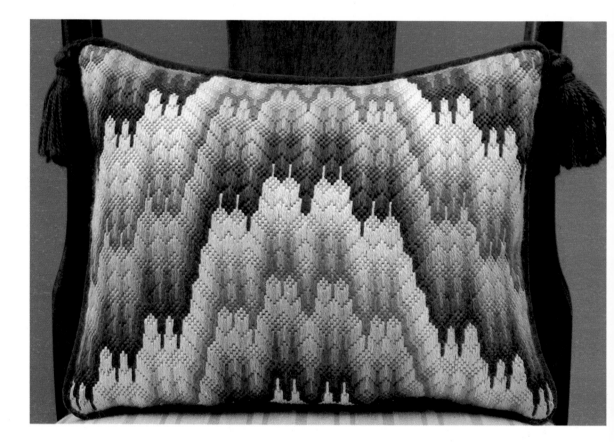

BLUE-RUST FLORENTINE PILLOW

Finished size: 14" × 10¾"
Materials: #13 tan mono canvas
#20 tapestry needle
Persian yarn, 1 skein of each: 365–French
    Navy; 334–Dark French Blue; 385–
    French Blue; 756–Summer Blue;
    395–Light Blue; 414–Rust; 426–
    Glow; 425*–Indian Pink; 464–
    Orange Ice; 012–Ivory (* available
    in Paternayan only)
Fabric for pillow back: ½ yard
Note 1: If tassels are to be used (see Fin-
    ishing section), an extra skein of
    365–French Navy is needed.
Note 2: Separate the yarn and work with
    two-ply throughout.

Instructions: The pattern for the wing
chair is established by a long, wandering
line running from the center of the chair
back to the edge of the small wings. For
the pillow only the center section of the
chair back pattern is used. The chart
shows the full length of the Ivory row
that begins at the center of the piece and
establishes the pattern row. Once these
patterns are understood it is less confusing to have only the first row diagrammed. If you have never worked a
Florentine design, read pages 24–25 before beginning to work.

Tape the canvas and mark Lines *A*
and *B*. Beginning at the center with Ivory
yarn (012), place Stitch *a* on the vertical
line (Line *A*) with the bottom of the stitch
touching the horizontal (Line *B*). Following the chart, carefully count the row
from *a* to *b*. Fasten the yarn and begin
again at the center. Count the row to the
left edge reading the chart from *c* to *b*.
This completes Row 1, and all subsequent
rows can be worked across the canvas
from right to left.

Work downward using the colors in
order shading from Ivory to the deepest
Rust, then working from Light Blue
through the French Navy. In detail the
color order is as follows: 1 row of 012,
2 rows each in this sequence—464, 425,
426, 414, 395, 756, 385, 334, 365.

The bottom edge of the pillow is 2
threads below Stitch *d* on the chart. This
means that after 2 full rows have been
worked, only portions of the remainder
of rows will be needed to square the edge.

When the lower section has been
completed, turn the canvas and work 12
full rows (one complete repeat of the
blues plus 2 rows of 414–Rust). The ends
of the long stitches of the Rust row are
at the top edge of the pillow. Fill in with
short rows to complete section.

Block and construct pillow. Make
four tassels. Attach two in each of the
top corners.

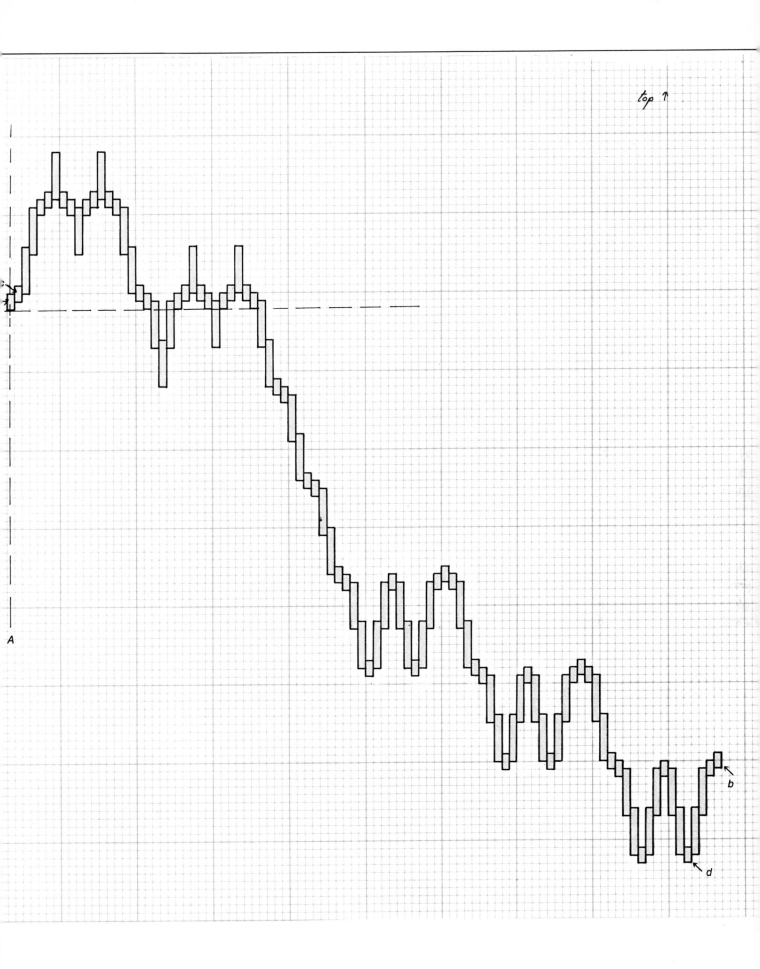

top ↑

A

b

d

PASTEL CHAIR SEAT

Bargello is an attractive and practical covering for seats of occasional and dining chairs. It is quickly finished, wears well, and has its own lovely distinction. This classic Queen Anne desk chair is covered in a traditional design worked in a whimsical blend of bright pastels. The combination works well because the chair is in a room that needs the pattern and the bright colors to offset a "too-planned" look.

Furniture dimensions vary so greatly that it would be impractical to write conventional directions for this chair and leave it at that. What follows is a description of the process for making this seat and suggestions for working independently to cover furniture of various sizes and styles.

This seat is worked on #17 cream mono canvas with two-ply Persian yarn. The canvas size is rather fine, but it was chosen to keep the scale of the pattern small and to maintain fairly short snag-proof stitches. The yarn colors are shades of pink, blue, yellow, peach, lavender and green. Ivory is used as the palest row of each color band. The Florentine Flame design is a typical one covering a wide area and using stitches of two lengths. The long stitches are worked over 6 threads, the short ones over 2. Reading up or down the row the two long stitches are always over two short ones in the typical Florentine manner. The seat shown required 17 skeins of yarn, one of each shade listed in the working order below.

The chair seat itself measures 17¼" along the narrowest edge at the back, 22" at the front, and is 19" deep. To allow for new padding and adequate turnunder, the finished Bargello measures 19¼" at the back, 24" at the front, and is 21" deep.

Facing page: The bands of pastel shades that zigzag across the seat of the Queen Anne chair are very apparent in this closeup view of a small section of the canvas. Note that each color stripe begins with ivory and works progressively through stronger values of color for 4 rows. The pattern could be worked in any number of combinations to fit special color schemes, as it is very versatile and adaptable.

PASTEL CHAIR SEAT

(Two inches were added to each measurement.) This outline was marked on a canvas 25″ × 28″ to allow a 2″ unworked border on all sides. The canvas was left rectangular until after blocking, when the excess canvas at the sides was trimmed, leaving 2″ borders on all sides.

To determine the correct size for the Bargello for your chair, measure the seat accurately and add 2″ to each measurement. In addition, allow at least a 2″ border of unworked canvas on all sides. Leave the canvas square or rectangular. Divide the canvas in half, with a vertical line running from the back to the front of the seat. The line is shown by the dashed Line A on the chart.

The chart for the Flame line can be used for various-size chairs. It is such a long line, and the colors are so many, that it is best worked by placing the point of the Flame at Stitch *a* on the marked center line at the back of the seat and counting as many repeats as necessary to the side edges. To begin, work from *a* to *b*, reading the chart from left to right; then read the chart from *c* back toward *a* until the line reaches the marked edge of the canvas at the right. Repeat the process to establish the other half of the first row to the left side. All subsequent rows can be worked across the canvas in one operation. As the width of the seat increases, continue the established pattern outward.

Row 1, which is shown on the chart, is Ivory. Working down from the top of the canvas use the colors in the following order: 012, Ivory, 1 row (already worked); 831–Pale Pink, 1 row; 641–Light Mauve, 2 rows; 631–Light Iris, 1 row; 012–Ivory, 1 row; 831–Pale Pink, 1 row; 865–Powder Pink, 2 rows; 860–Magnolia, 1 row; 012–Ivory, 1 row; 458–Daffodil, 1 row; 456–Baby Yellow, 2 rows; 450–Yellow, 1 row; 012–Ivory, 1 row; 395–Light Blue, 3 rows; 756–Summer Blue, 1 row; 012–Ivory, 1 row; 464–Orange Ice, 1 row; 454–Pale Pumpkin, 2 rows; 988–Peach, 1 row; 012–Ivory, 1 row; 575–Spring Pea Green, 1 row; 570–Celery Leaf, 2 rows; 555–Green Giant, 1 row. Repeat the color sequence as often as necessary.

Note that because of the number of colors used, the repeat will not work out so that every Ivory row has the same stitch configuration as the charted row. It will be 19 rows before that happens again, but this is not a problem. Just work downward using the colors in order and maintaining the rhythm of two long stitches above two short ones and everything will work out perfectly.

If canvas with a mesh larger than the #17 pictured is used, the size of the Flame and the length of the stitches will increase in proportion to the increase in mesh size.

This design is also handsome worked either in a monochromatic color scheme or in a combination of two contrasting colors. One of the most intriguing aspects of Bargello design is the great changes that can be wrought with color variations.

The task of fastening the finished Bargello to a slip seat is not difficult. Trim the blocked piece, leaving at least 2″ of unworked canvas on all sides. Center the pattern on the seat and staple or tack it securely in place mitering the corners to assure a good fit. Cover the entire back with a piece of muslin to hide the tacks and raw canvas edges.

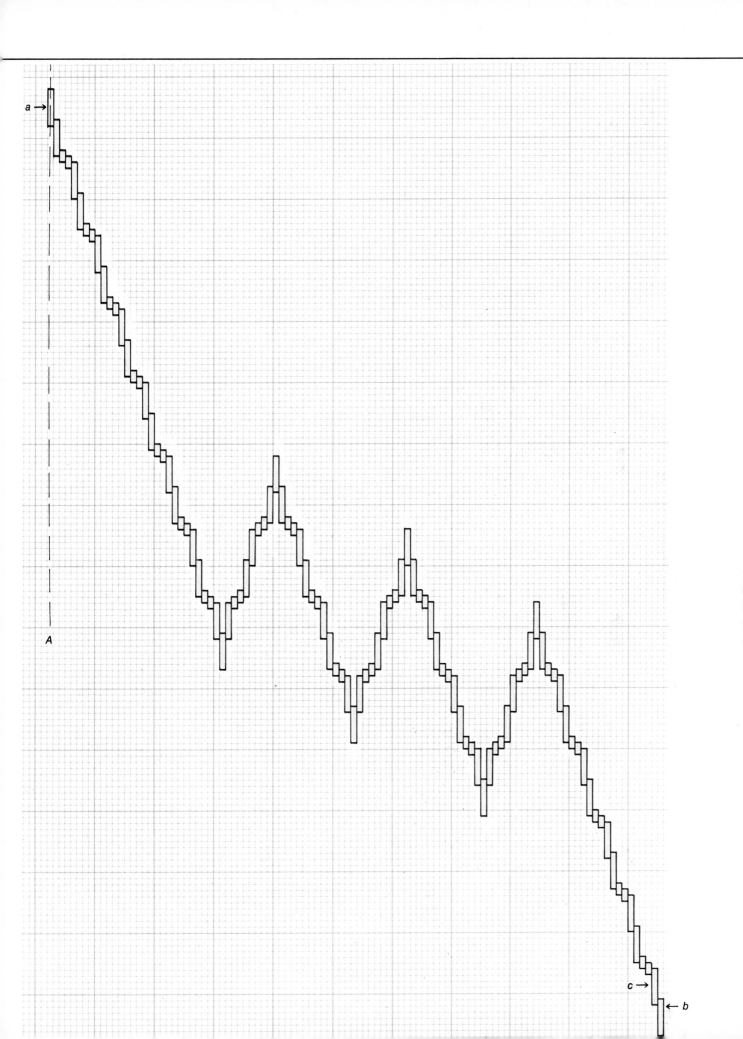

GOLD CHAIR

To undertake to make upholstery fabric for a chair is an ambitious project, but Bargello's long, quick stitches make it an attainable goal. This small wing chair is covered entirely in Bargello—even the back—but the work could have been reduced a great deal if the back and sides had been upholstered in matching velveteen. This would make the undertaking even more reasonable.

The canvas is a fine-quality #14 white mono weave which is woven 60" wide especially for large projects. This width can be cut to good advantage and eliminates piecing large sections. The size of the mesh is appropriate for upholstery, as the long stitches work up quickly but are not so long that they are prone to snagging and pulling.

The yarn used is a fine-quality wool in four shades of bright gold. To make the pattern stripes wide and to emphasize the lighter values of gold, the pale shades are repeated more than once. There are 3 rows of the lightest gold, 2 of the next deeper tone, and only 1 each of the medium and dark gold. There is a delicate blending of values from light to dark, but the overall color of the chair is much paler than it would be if there had been 1 row of each shade to each repeat.

The design for the Bargello is a Florentine Flame which meanders from the center of the chair back to the edge of the wings. The long stitches are worked over six threads, the short ones over two. The center portion of the design has been charted on page 37 and has been worked in a different color combination to make the Blue-Rust Pillow also shown there.

To upholster the average wing chair requires 6 to 7 yards of 54" fabric. Obviously there is some waste, so it would

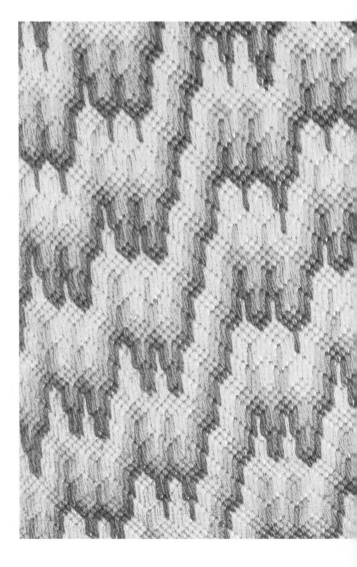

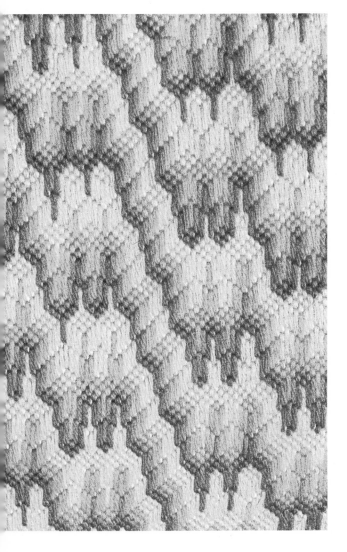

Left: This closeup detail of the center back of the wing chair shows part of the repeat of the pattern. The chart on page 37 shows the first row. The long stitches in the design are worked over 6 threads, the short ones over 2. Size-14-mesh canvas keeps the long stitches a length practical for upholstery—long enough to be quick to work, short enough to be snag-free.

GOLD CHAIR

be impractical to make the straight yardage. Better to make a muslin pattern and work the individual pieces, centering the design on each and avoiding waste. For most furniture this requires expertise in the planning stages; if possible, it is best to have a professional cut the muslin.

After the muslin pieces are cut, lay them out on the canvas and trace around them with a waterproof pen allowing at least 1½" on all sides. In addition, leave borders to be unworked 3 to 4" if possible. If a piece is irregular in shape, trace and work the necessary shape but leave the canvas rectangular or square so it can be blocked. The upholsterer will trim it as needed.

Buy all the canvas for the chair at once, as slight variations in weave may be obvious when the Bargello is finished. It is difficult to estimate the quantities of yarn that will be needed; but you can make a reasonable guess based on experience, then quickly work one section, keeping track of the yarn used and compute from that an approximation. Buy more yarn than the estimated need. Extra can be used for accent pieces in the room with the chair or it can be returned or exchanged. Be aware that the project could take a long time to complete and nothing could be more devastating than to have a chair almost finished, need more of a color, and find it has been discontinued.

Some of the pieces will be large and unwieldy, others small and portable. Work on two at once—keep a big one at home and a little one in a work bag ready to travel. That way the project moves along fast.

Be wary about dividing the work among family and friends to speed finishing. Differences in working methods and stitch tension may show when the pieces are assembled. This is not to say that it never works—just to indicate that there may be problems. I was lucky. My elder daughter, who works much like me, was willing to work a great deal of the embroidery, and our work is so much alike that we can't identify which pieces we did.

For a project like this only the best possible materials should be used to make the time involved well invested. The total for yarn and canvas will compare to the purchase of a fine upholstery fabric, but the Bargello will probably never have to be replaced. Professional upholsterers' labor charges are the same for needlepoint as for fabric. Don't try to put a monetary value on the time spent—charge it to recreation and forget it.

Care for the chair as you would for any piece of fine upholstered furniture. You may wish to have the Bargello treated with one of the stain repellents as a precaution. The embroidery seems to improve with the years, developing the soft patina that comes to good furniture that is used daily and well cared for.

To adapt this design for another chair, use the chart on page 37 and repeat as much as necessary of the line on each canvas section. The design should be centered on most of the pieces—match the back, cushions, box sections for the pillow, and the fronts carefully. If the wings of your chair are separate pieces, match the horizontal pattern to that of the back section so the pattern is carried across correctly.

To work in the colors shown on the finished chair use the colors in the following order: 3 rows 467–Light Medium Yellow; 2 rows 441–Medium Yellow; 1 row 447–Mustard; 1 row 427–Medium Gold.

NEEDLEPOINT AND CREWELPOINT

COLONIAL SAMPLER TOTE

Plastic canvas, a marvel of modern technology, provides the firm but flexible foundation for this handsome carryall or purse. The mesh size is a comfortable 7 to the inch, which translates the traditional sampler designs into bright graphics.

Two color variations illustrate the changes possible just by substituting a two-color scheme for the bright multicolor version. Your imagination has probably already suggested ways to use your own favorite colors.

Finished size: 13½″ × 10½″ × 2½″

Materials: Plastic "canvas" sheets
    (10½″ × 13½″)—3 pieces

#18 tapestry needle

Fabric for lining: ½ yard

Ribbon for handle facings: 1 yard, ½″
    wide

Persian yarn as follows: 520–Hunter
    Green, 5 skeins; 843–Fireball, 1
    skein; 452–Light Yellow, 1 skein;
    012–Ivory, 3 skeins; 742–True Blue,
    1 skein

Navy version: 365–French Navy, 5
    skeins; 005–White, 3 skeins

Note 1: Four-ply knitting-worsted-weight
    yarn—either wool or synthetic—
    may be substituted for the Persian
    yarn at considerable saving. One
    4-ounce skein of each of the main
    colors (green and ivory, or navy and
    white) will be sufficient. For the multicolor
    version only small amounts
    of the other colors are needed and
    can be either knitting yarn or Persian.

Note 2: If working with Persian yarn, add
    an extra ply and work with a four-ply
    strand for better coverage.

Instructions: The plastic sheets are 70 holes by 90 holes. For the front and back sections use one full sheet each. Cut the remaining sheet as follows to make pieces for the sides, bottom, and handles: two side panels 70 × 20; one piece 90 × 20 for bottom; two pieces 70 × 5 for the handles. See cutting diagram for layout. Count holes when cutting the sections.

Work the patterned sections for the front, back, and sides in the Half Cross Stitch. Yarn quantities have been based on the use of this stitch, and a change to another stitch may cause a shortage of yarn. Work on the plastic mesh as if it were canvas on a stretcher frame, making each stitch with an up-and-down motion rather than trying to "sew" the stitch in a single thrust. The plastic is flexible, but not pliable enough to allow the needle to pass in and out in a single stroke as is usual on canvas.

Work the front, back, and two side panels in the pattern as charted. Work the bottom section in Brick Stitch in Hunter Green.

Cutting Diagram

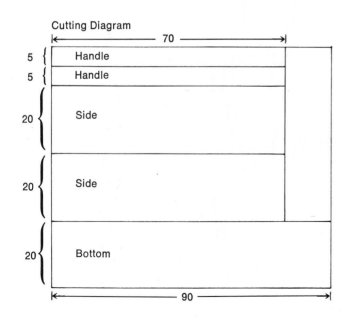

5 {	Handle	
5 {	Handle	
20 {	Side	
20 {	Side	
20 {	Bottom	

70

90

COLONIAL SAMPLER TOTE

With Ivory work a row of Upright Gobelin Stitch over three bars down the center of the handle pieces. Using a double strand of green, overcast the edges to cover the exposed bar.

Using the plastic pieces as a pattern, cut the lining, adding ⅝" seam allowances on all sides. Sew seams. Press. Turn the seam allowance at top edge of lining to wrong side and press it in place.

Matching the holes of the adjoining pieces, join the bag sections with an overcasting stitch and a double strand of background yarn. Finish the top edge of the bag with the same overcasting stitch. Attach the bag handles, centering them over the tree motifs in the border pattern. Whip ribbon over wrong side of handles. Allow ends of ribbon to extend down into bag. Lining will cover them.

Insert lining and fasten it along the top of the bag with invisible stitches into the overcasting stitches.

Side Panel

Center row—do not repeat

520   843   452   012   742

Front and Back

BARGELLO AND MACRAMÉ HANGING

The recent revival of the ancient craft of macramé has introduced many to this fascinating textile art in which a few basic knots deftly combined create beautiful patterns and textures. Macramé articles range from the simplest knotted plant hanger to elaborate wall hangings and textile "sculptures" of museum quality.

This interesting bell pull or hanging is an unlikely combination of a small Bargello panel and a long macramé fringe. The Bargello is an oblong Four-way design with two circular cutouts behind which hangs a sennit of four widely spaced Square Knots. The long macramé section is a relatively easy combination of the Square Knot and the Half Hitch worked in the most important color of the Persian yarn used in the Bargello. The result is an elegant contemporary piece. (Those unfamiliar with knots should consult a macramé book.)

Finished size: Overall: 5¾″ × 34½″
Bargello: 5¾″ × 10½″
Macramé: 5¾″ × 24″
Materials: #13 tan mono canvas approximately 10″ × 14½″
#20 tapestry needle
Persian yarn as follows: 248*–Deep Ash Rose, 100 yards; 430*–Medium Ash Rose, 5 yards; 287*–Light Ash Rose, 5 yards; 020–Neutral, 1 skein; 012–Ivory, 1 skein (* available in Paternayan only)
Medium-weight iron-on interfacing 5¾″ × 10½″
Appropriate lining fabric 5¾″ × 10½″
Metal picture hanger with serrated edge
Note: Separate the yarn and work the Bargello two-ply. Use yarn full-ply for the macramé.

Instructions: Tape the canvas and mark with Lines *A* and *B*. Measure up from the bottom edge of the canvas 4¾″ along the vertical Line *A* and mark. Working diagonally out from this mark to the lower corners, place the two miter lines for the lower half of the piece as indicated on the chart. (The chart shows only the lower right quarter; the remaining two miter lines at the top can be easily marked with a minimum of counting after the first row is worked.)

With color 012, start Row 1 by placing Stitch *a* in the mesh in which the miter lines intersect the vertical line (Line *A*). Counting carefully, work to Stitch *b* on the miter line. Turn the canvas (and the chart) clockwise a quarter-turn and continue the row to Stitch *c* on the horizontal line (Line *B*). Continue the line from *c* back to *b* once more to complete one long side. Mark another miter line along the diagonal into which Stitch *b* is worked. Turn the canvas and work a short row, following the chart from *b* to *a* and back to *b*. Mark the fourth miter line through the mesh at *b*. Turn the canvas another quarter-turn and repeat the long side. Turn the canvas again and finish the short side, reading the chart from *b* to *a*.

Following the chart, complete the Ivory outlines of the motifs. Fill in, placing the colors as shown on the chart. Complete the background, maintaining the stitching pattern established by the outline of the design. Following the outline of the first Ivory row, work a row of Deep Ash Rose around the two circular center motifs. Leave the balance of these sections unworked. Finish the edges of the piece with a row of Gobelin Stitch

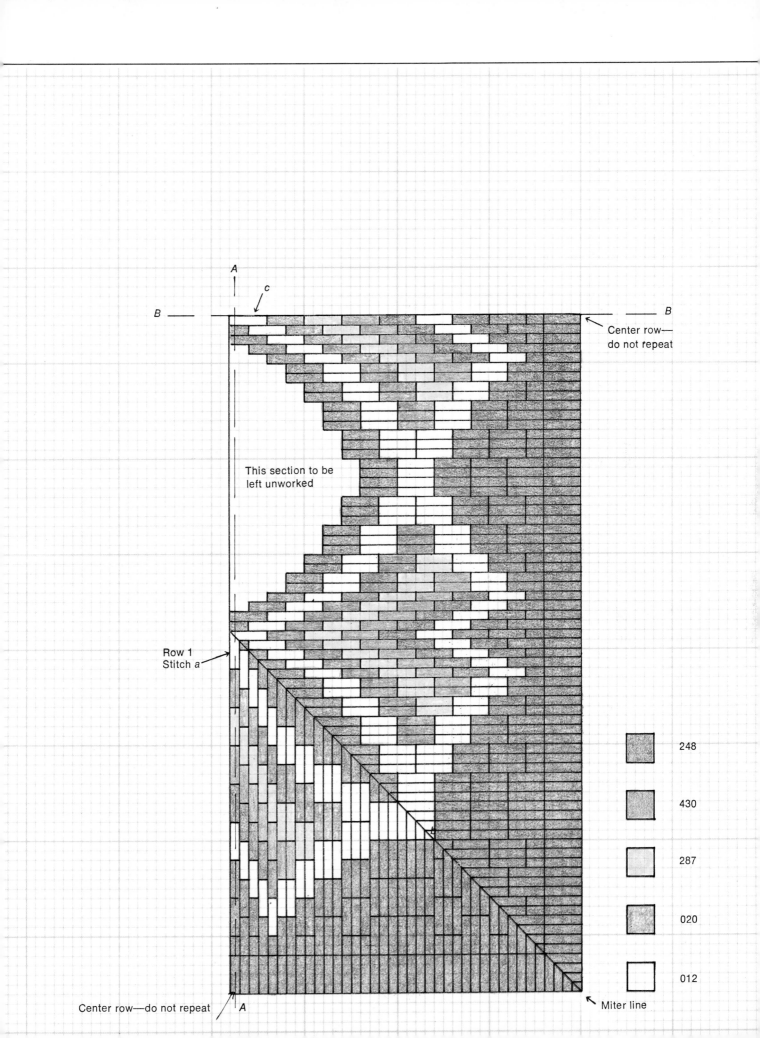

A

c

B ————— B

Center row—
do not repeat

This section to be
left unworked

Row 1
Stitch a

248

430

287

020

012

Center row—do not repeat

A

Miter line

BARGELLO AND MACRAMÉ HANGING

worked over 4 threads to form a border. With a single strand of matching yarn, work a row of Back Stitch between the row of Gobelin Stitch and the body of the piece.

Block. Trim the canvas borders to ½" and press to wrong side, mitering corners neatly. Do not cut out unworked circular canvas sections. Rather, clip from the center to the edge of the Bargello stitches, leaving pie-shaped wedges. Pull the wedge-shaped pieces to the wrong side and press into place. To avoid any raw edges of the canvas showing, turn back a small portion of the Bargello stitches with the canvas.

Cut the interfacing slightly smaller than the Bargello and fuse the two together according to the instructions for the interfacing. Using the Bargello as a guide, cut lining, allowing ⅝" hem allowances on all edges. Press these allowances to the wrong side.

Cut four 12" strands of color 248. Make sennit by tying two Square Knots about 2" from top, skipping 1" and making two Square Knots, skipping ⅝", and tying two Square Knots, skipping 1" and tying two Square Knots. Glue sennit to back of Bargello panel with knots spaced evenly within the cutouts.

For the macramé section cut 28 2½-yard lengths of Persian yarn, color 248. Knot over a 10" length of yarn to make 56 ends. Working across the row using groups of 4 threads, make 14 Square Knots. Repeat once. Skip down 1" and work 2 rows of horizontal Half Hitches. Follow with a row of 14 twisted sennits of 20 Half Knots each. Next work a row of horizontal Half Hitches.

To begin the V-shaped Square Knot section, make a row of Square Knots across the 56 ends. Omitting 2 threads at the beginning and end of the first row and 2 more at each end of every following row, work Square Knots down until one knot is formed at center. Go back to the top of the "V" and, with the four outside cords on each side, work two Square Knots. Skip 1" and work two Square Knots. Repeat until there are six groups of knots on each sennit.

On the remaining 48 threads skip down 2" and tie a row of diagonal Half Hitches outlining the "V." Skip 2" and work a row of twisted sennits of 20 knots each. Skip 2" and work a row of diagonal Half Hitches.

Using all 56 ends, tie 14 Square Knot sennits each four knots in length. Work a row of diagonal Half Hitches. Repeat the Square Knot sennits of four knots each. Finish the panel with 2 rows of diagonal Half Hitches. Trim the fringe to follow the diagonal lines, leaving it as long as possible.

With matching sewing thread and invisible stitches, attach the macramé to the bottom of the Bargello panel. Hand-sew the lining to the panel. Sew the picture hanger to the top.

The sizing of the tan mono canvas used for the model was sufficient to allow the above construction method and produce a panel that hangs well. If your canvas seems softer or the sizing has disappeared during the working, use a heavier-weight interfacing or mount the Bargello panel over a cardboard backing.

Complete beginner macramé instructions are outside the scope of this book. If you have never attempted macramé, consult a basic instruction book and learn the knots with practice cord. Those familiar with macramé knots and technique will find the hanging easy to make.

EXERCISE SANDALS

When one of the straps of the exercise sandals finally wore out, the wooden soles were still capable of much mileage. New needlepoint bands adorned with an Apache beadwork design in typical Indian colors renewed the sandals and made them even better-looking than before.

The Apache design can be used thus on the sandals, but is also an excellent one for belts, luggage or camera straps, glasses cases, or as a Cross Stitch border design.

Finished size: 2¾" × 7¼" (length will vary according to the width of shoe being fitted)
Materials: #14 white mono canvas approximately 6" × 22"
#20 tapestry needle
Persian yarn as follows: 365–French Blue, 5 yards; 456–Baby Yellow, 5 yards; 510–Medium Green, 5 yards; 252–Red, 5 yards; 005–White, 1 skein
Lining fabric approximately 6" × 22"
Note: Separate the yarn and work with two-ply throughout.

Instructions: Cut the canvas into two pieces 6" × 11" and tape the edges. The dashed lines on the chart indicate the approximate shape of the sandal strap. This will vary slightly for individual pairs of shoes. To make certain that the finished needlepoint will fit like the original leather strap, remove the old strap and use it as a pattern for drawing the diagonal lines which form the side edges. The width of the strap is that of the design area plus 3 rows on either side of the widest point.

Center the pattern on the marked section of the canvas and work entirely in Tent Stitch. Begin working at the center and continue outward until all of the color design is worked. Finish the strap by working the white background. Check the size of this first strap and make any adjustment necessary before making the second one.

Block completed straps. Trim canvas borders to ½" and use trimmed needlepoint as a pattern for cutting lining pieces. With right sides together, sew linings to the needlepoint, leaving most of one long side open. Trim seams, cutting close to the stitching at the corners. Turn. Press. Turn seam allowances of opening to inside and slipstitch to close seam.

Attach to sandal using the original screws. If the screws do not pass through the needlepoint easily, use a small awl or the point of the embroidery scissors to make an opening between the needlepoint stitches.

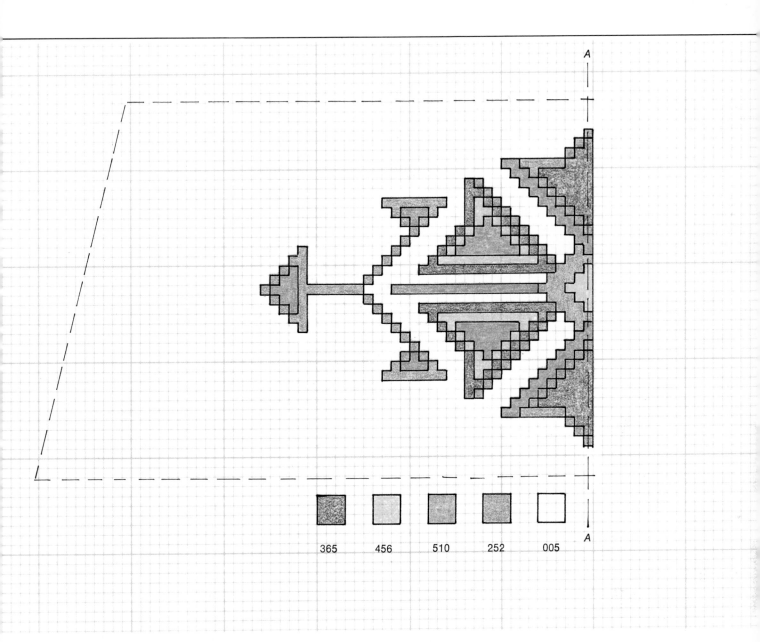

365	456	510	252	005

PANSY PICTURE

Stylized pansies and bright pastels make a picture as bright as a springtime garden. The Basket Weave Stitch and #10 canvas make this a quickly finished piece, while the textured stitches on the pansy faces allow for experimentation with crewel stitches on needlepoint. The embroidery stitches are only three—Bullion, French Knots, and Straight Stitch—but the effect is charming.

The 14" square size of the piece makes it perfect for use as a pillow if desired. Finish with self-cording and a back in one of the pastel shades to make a gay accent for any room.

Finished size: 14" × 14"
Materials: #10 white interlocking canvas
    18" × 18"
#18 tapestry needle
Persian yarn, 1 skein except as noted:
    631–Light Iris; 641–Light Mauve;
    865–Powder Pink; 452–Light Yel-
    low; 458–Daffodil; G64–Apple
    Spring Green; G74–Light Apple
    Green; 005–White; 050–Black;
    395–Light Blue, 2 skeins
Framing materials or ½ yard appropriate
    fabric if piece is finished as a pillow.
Note: Use yarn full-ply, as it comes from
    the skein, for both needlepoint and
    embroidery.

Instructions: Tape the canvas and trace the design onto it. Begin working at center and work outward, first outlining a flower in Black and then filling in the area with the color specified. Work the Tent Stitch to the edges of the irregularly shaped details at flower centers. Leave these portions unworked until all the needlepoint has been completed.

The closeup photograph shown here and the stitch detail on page 149 show the finished appearance of the pansy faces.

Closeup of the pansies shows massed pastel flowers and leaves outlined in black. The embroidery stitches for centers and "whiskers" add slight texture. There is another detail photograph of this piece among the canvas stitch illustrations at the back of the book.

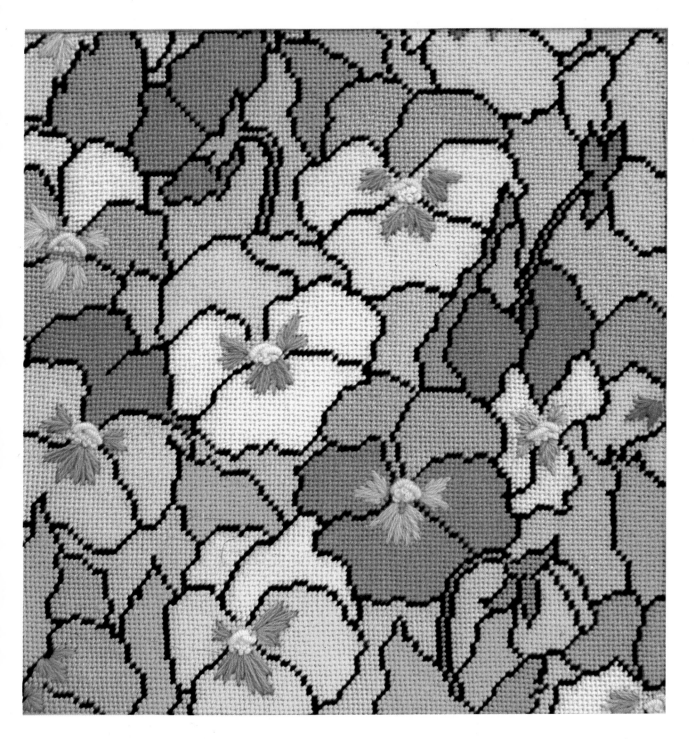

Work the embroidery stitches exactly as on other fabrics, allowing the stitches to overlap onto the needlepoint so all canvas is covered. Work the "whiskers" in Straight Stitches of varying lengths as shown in the detail photograph. Overlap and work some on top of others to achieve a raised look. Place the French Knots close together in a cluster; work two Bullion Stitches at the top of the cluster.

Block and frame as shown or make into a pillow.

PANSY PICTURE

Top left

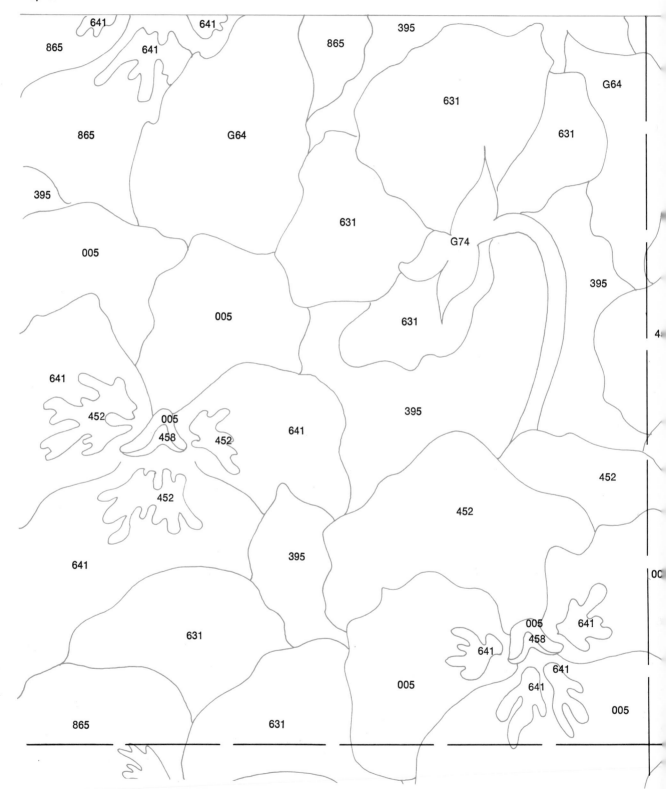

Note: Fold your tracing paper in quarters, then open it
flat and match the fold lines to the dashed lines on the
charts here through page 61

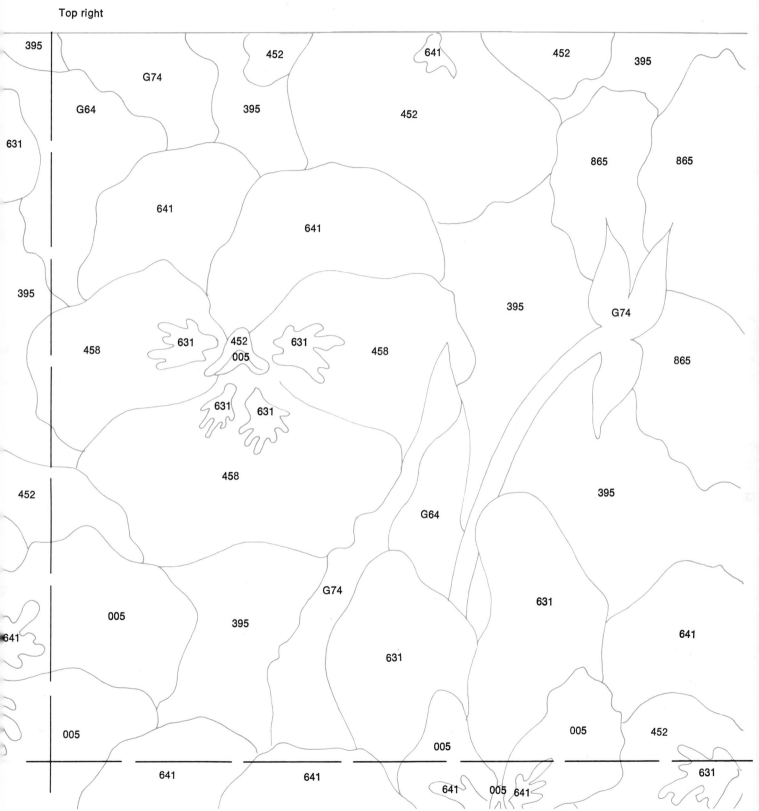

PANSY PICTURE

Bottom left

Bottom right

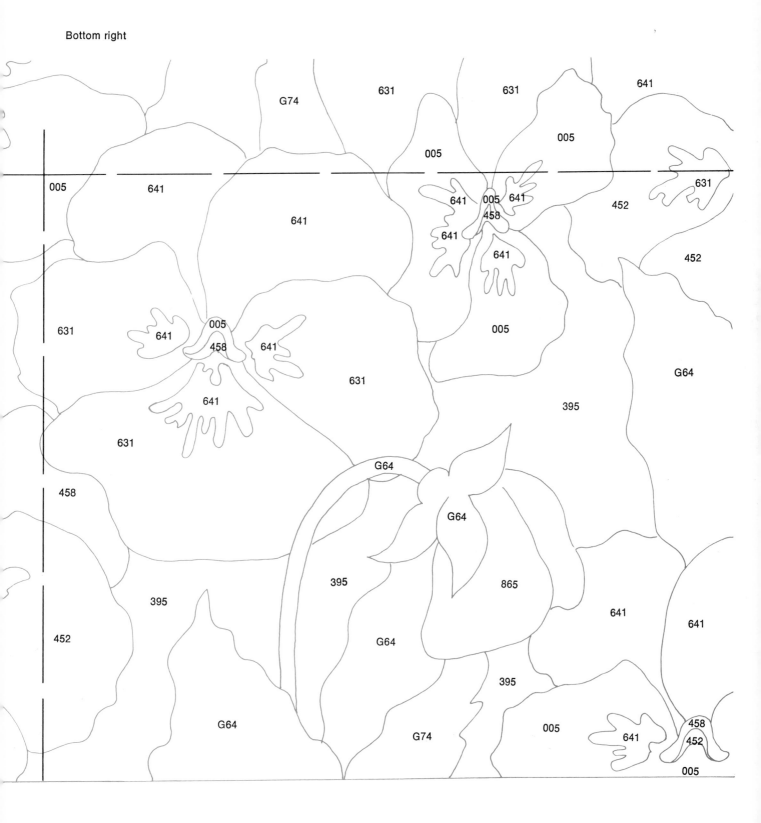

NOSTALGIC PASTEL PILLOW

Delicate, dainty, sweet, feminine, poetic, nostalgic—words not ordinarily applicable to Bargello's geometric patterns are the best for this unusual pillow. The colors are the palest pastels that could be found, and the three designs decorated with touches of embroidery are perfectly adapted small-scale patterns that work out well in the pale colors. Portions of design filled in with Tent Stitch form a contrasting background for the stylized Satin Stitch flowers that accentuate the feminine feeling.

The three design areas are separated by bands of Gobelin Stitch border worked in various stitch lengths and in different color arrangements. The borders have an interesting padded and raised effect that results from working the Gobelin Stitch over a three-ply traumé thread of the same-color yarn (see p. 146). Then when a row of Back Stitch is worked between the Gobelin rows, the raised look gains prominence, producing a quilted look.

Finished size: 14½″ × 14½″
Materials: #14 white mono canvas approximately 18½″ × 18½″
#20 tapestry needle
Persian yarn as follows: 765–Light Teal, 2 skeins; 831–Pale Pink, 2 skeins; 458–Daffodil, 2 skeins; 641–Light Mauve, 1 skein; 566–Iced Green, 1 skein; 005–White, 3 skeins
Fabric for pillow back: ½ yard
Note 1: Separate the yarn and work Bargello, Tent, and embroidery stitches with two-ply.
Note 2: Embroidery stitches are worked on top of the completed Tent Stitch areas.

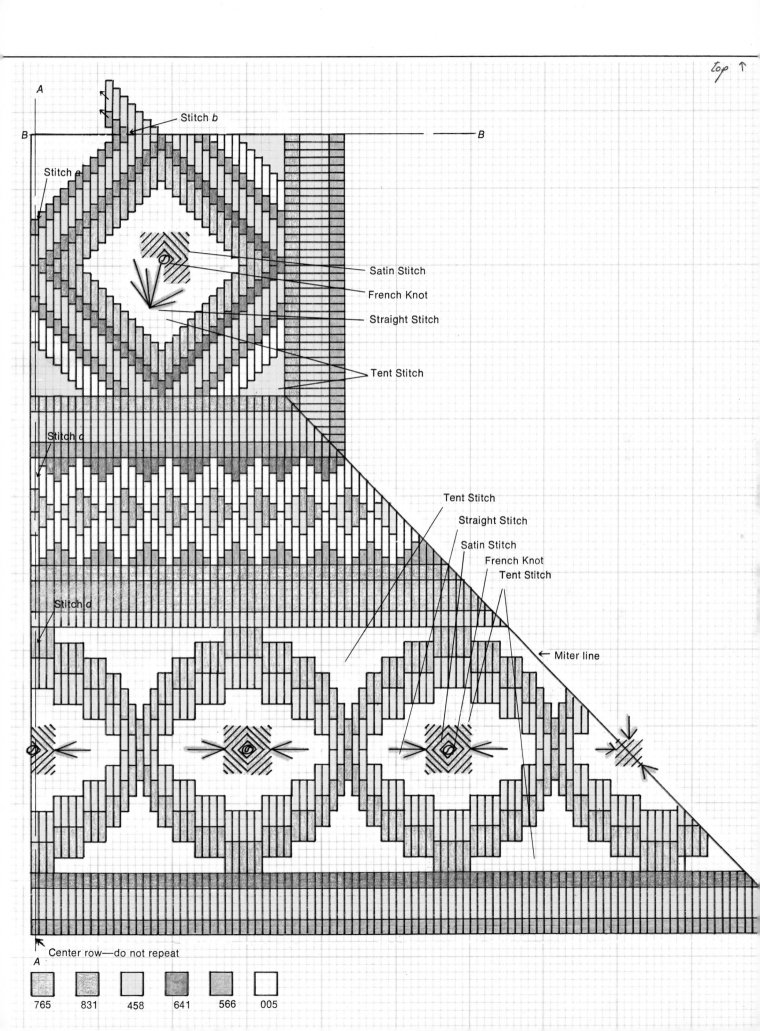

top ↑

A

B ──────────────────────────────── B

Stitch b

Stitch a

Satin Stitch

French Knot

Straight Stitch

Tent Stitch

Stitch c

Stitch d

Tent Stitch

Straight Stitch

Satin Stitch

French Knot

Tent Stitch

← Miter line

Center row—do not repeat

A

| 765 | 831 | 458 | 641 | 566 | 005 |

NOSTALGIC PASTEL PILLOW

Instructions: Tape the canvas and mark with Lines *A, B, C,* and *D* as for Four-way Bargello. The miter lines are not used for the center panel, but are best marked out from the center before work has begun.

Begin working on the center panel. From the intersection of lines count down 11 mesh in Line *A* and place the top of Stitch *a* in that mesh. Working to the right, count 13 stitches, ending with Stitch *b* on the horizontal center line. Continuing in the direction noted by the arrows, work the balance of the center diamond shape. Outline the diamond with another diamond in yellow (Daffodil) with stitches 4 threads long as shown. Working outward, outline the lavender (Light Mauve) diamonds and continue until the five Bargello diamonds are completed. Fill in the partial diamonds at the sides as shown. Work the plain areas on the chart in Tent Stitch in white and yellow as shown.

Embroider the five flowers centered on the Tent Stitch diamonds in padded Satin Stitch, slanting the stitches in the direction of the lines on the flower on the chart. The center is a French Knot; the leaves are Straight Stitch.

Edge the completed square with 3 rows of Gobelin Stitch border in the stitch lengths and colors shown. To achieve the padded look, work the Gobelin Stitches over a three-ply traumé thread and work a row of Back Stitch with a single strand of matching yarn between the rows of Gobelin Stitch.

Work the inner Bargello border beginning with Stitch *c* on the center line. Count to the miter line, turn the canvas, and work to the next miter, continuing around the square until the row joins at *c*.

Complete the section using colors as indicated. Outline with Gobelin rows and Back Stitch as in first border.

Begin blue (Light Teal) Bargello outlines at Stitch *d* and work around the piece turning at miter lines to complete row completely around the square. Complete both blue and yellow Bargello rows, then fill in the spaces shown as plain white areas with Tent Stitch. Embroider the flowers in positions shown, slanting the Satin Stitch in the direction of the lines on the flowers. Centers are French Knots; leaves are Straight Stitch.

Complete the last border in the colors shown working over a traumé thread and finishing with Back Stitch as in previous borders. Block and construct pillow.

Facing page: Use this detail of part of the center square in combination with the chart to set up the diamond outlines. The dainty pink flowers worked in padded Satin Stitch are slightly raised. There is a detail photograph of the outer border of the pillow among the canvas stitch illustrations at the back of the book.

FLORAL STRIPE PILLOW

Needlepoint, crewel, and Bargello combine here on a fine-mesh canvas to make a lovely and intricate piece of embroidery. In a day when there is much emphasis on easy and quick projects, it is fun for a change to work on a challenging piece that is not finished overnight. The fine-count canvas does make the needlepoint sections time-consuming, but the Bargello saves much time and adds an interesting textured background.

The outlines of the crewel flowers are traced on the canvas, the Tent Stitch worked right to the lines, then the embroidery worked so the stitches overlap into the needlepoint. This covers the canvas well and imparts to the embroidery a raised look. The texture of the Bargello is a pleasant contrast to the tiny, flat needlepoint, but its single pale color prevents its overpowering the delicate floral embroidery.

This piece can be modified for use as an oblong stool top by eliminating the Gobelin borders and extending the Bargello to the necessary size. If a change of background color is needed, the flowers will be equally lovely on white, ivory, black, pale green, grey, blue, or medium rose.

Finished size: 13" × 14½"
Materials: #17 cream mono canvas approximately 17" × 18½"
#24 tapestry needle
Persian yarn as follows: 467–Light Medium Yellow, 5 skeins; and about 15 yards of each of the following for embroidery: 510–Medium Green; 334–Dark French Blue; 385–French Blue; 395–Light Blue; 205–Reddish Brown; 281–Antique Pink; 865–Powder Pink
Fabric for pillow back: ½ yard

Facing page: Closeup of one of the floral stripes shows in detail the embroidery and the texture of the one-color Bargello. Work the flowers as shown, using the lightest shades of the rose and blue at the outside of the petals and working through the values to the darkest at the base of the flowers. Overlap the embroidery stitches into the petit point background.

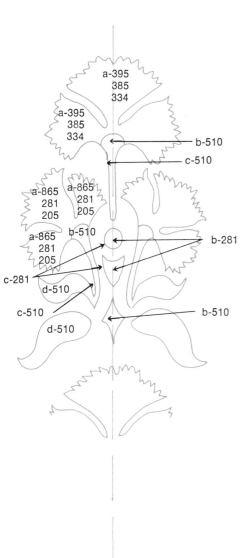

a-395
385
334

a-395
385
334

b-510

c-510

a-865
281
205

a-865
281
205

a-865
281
205

b-510

b-281

c-281

d-510

c-510

b-510

d-510

Stitches

a–Long-and-Short
b–Satin
c–Outline
d–Fishbone

FLORAL STRIPE PILLOW

Note: Separate the yarn and use two-ply for the Bargello, one strand for the Tent Stitch and the embroidery.

Instructions: This piece consists of three embroidered needlepoint sections on a background of four Bargello panels. Three rows of Gobelin Stitch of varying lengths form a textured self-border. Lay out the design following the steps outlined below in careful sequence.

Tape the canvas and draw the vertical line (Line *A*) down the middle. On Line *A* measure down 4" from the taped edge at the top of the canvas. Begin Row 1 with Stitch *a* at this point and work carefully across the row to Stitch *b* at the right, noting the change from the 4–2 step scallop to the Florentine Stitch pattern. Fasten the yarn at *b* and begin again at center. Skipping center Stitch *a*, repeat the line to the left side and end yarn. This row establishes the stitching pattern for the panels and outlines the curve at the top of the needlepoint sections.

Draw a 10" vertical line down from the center Stitch *c* at the top of each of the side scallops. This line corresponds to the dashed lines (one of these, Line *A*, is of course already drawn) shown on the chart. The line marking the center of the piece is already drawn through the center of the middle section.

Draw a vertical line on a sheet of parchment or vellum. Place paper over the drawing of the floral motif and trace. Using the partial center flower shown as a spacing aid, trace the motif twice more to form the stripe pattern. Make the outlines heavy enough to be visible through the canvas.

Place the tracing of the floral stripe under the canvas matching the vertical lines and having the top of the first flower 1/2" below the Bargello Stitches *a* and *c*.

Trace the flowers onto the canvas. Repeat for the remaining two panels. Draw a horizontal line across the canvas at a point 1 1/2" below the diamond at base of last floral motif. This marks the bottom edge of the piece—exclusive of the Gobelin borders. Draw another horizontal line across the top of the canvas in the row of mesh intersected by Stitch *b* at the edges. This line marks the top of the piece.

The canvas is now marked and ready to have work begin. Complete the Bargello background from Row 1 to the top edge. Work the sections—denoted by the solid lines between the panels on the chart—separately for best results, as the patterns are not continuous and the transition can be confusing. Notes on the chart are meant to aid in setting up the pattern and to make the instructions clear.

Discontinue the scallop pattern, but continue the Florentine Stitch panels to the marked line at the bottom. These panels need not be completed at once. As soon as enough of the panels has been worked to establish the side borders of the needlepoint sections, the Tent stitch can be started. Work in Basket Weave and work right up to or slightly over the outlines for the embroidery. At a point 1/2" below the lower floral motif begin the scallop Bargello pattern again to echo the arched shape of the top of the panel. Work this pattern to the line marking the bottom of the piece.

After all Bargello and needlepoint is completed, embroider the flowers, noting in the color photograph the alternating arrangement of the colors. Work the flowers in Long-and-Short Stitch, beginning with the lightest shade at the outside edge and shading to the deepest hue at the center. The chart and the detail photograph show a group of flowers with the larger center flower worked in blue. In the alternate arrangement, when the pink flower is in the center, the colors are the same, only placed differently. Use the detail photograph as a guide for embroidery. Work all embroidery just as on fabric, and overlap the stitches onto the needlepoint to assure good canvas coverage. Work heavily, placing stitches close together or on top of each other so the work has a padded, raised look.

The Gobelin border consists of 3 rows of varying widths which have been worked over a three-ply strand of yarn traumé-fashion for a corded look. To work, lay the yarn in place and work over it—the Gobelin Stitches hold it in place and conceal it. The stitches for the first border row should be over 4 threads. Follow with a row over 2 threads, and finish with a row 6 threads wide. With a single strand of yarn work a row of Back Stitch between the Gobelin rows. Block and construct pillow.

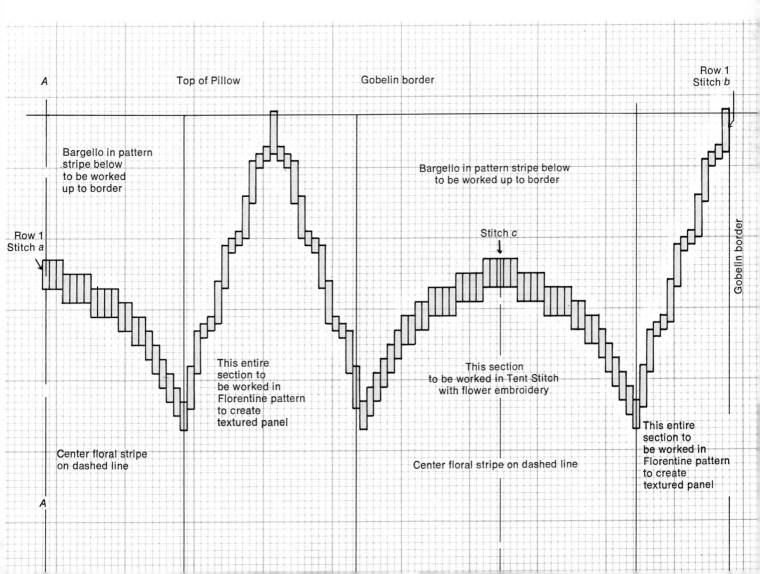

PASTEL SQUARE

A bevy of pastel pillows lavishly trimmed with lace, ruffles, and needlepoint adds the finishing feminine touch to a little girl's bed. The pillow in the photograph is appliquéd with a 5″ square of needlepoint combining Bargello with Tent Stitch and a few touches of embroidery.

Little pieces like this can also be used for pincushions, trivet inserts, or other items requiring a small square shape. The basic design idea inside the Gobelin borders can be multiplied to make a larger piece which can then be outlined with rows of Gobelin Stitch to form a border like the one used on the small piece.

Finished size: Needlepoint: 5″ × 5″
Pillow shown: 12½″ × 12½″

Materials: #14 white mono canvas approximately 9″ × 9″
#20 tapestry needle
Persian yarn, about 10 yards of each of the following: 756–Summer Blue; 831–Pale Pink; 458–Daffodil; G74–Light Apple Green; 005–White
White velveteen or uncut corduroy: ½ yard
Dacron quilt batting 13″ × 13″
Note: Separate the yarn and work needlepoint and embroidery with two strands.

Instructions: Tape the canvas and mark with the vertical and horizontal Lines *A* and *B* as for traditional Bargello. Count down 10 mesh from the intersection of

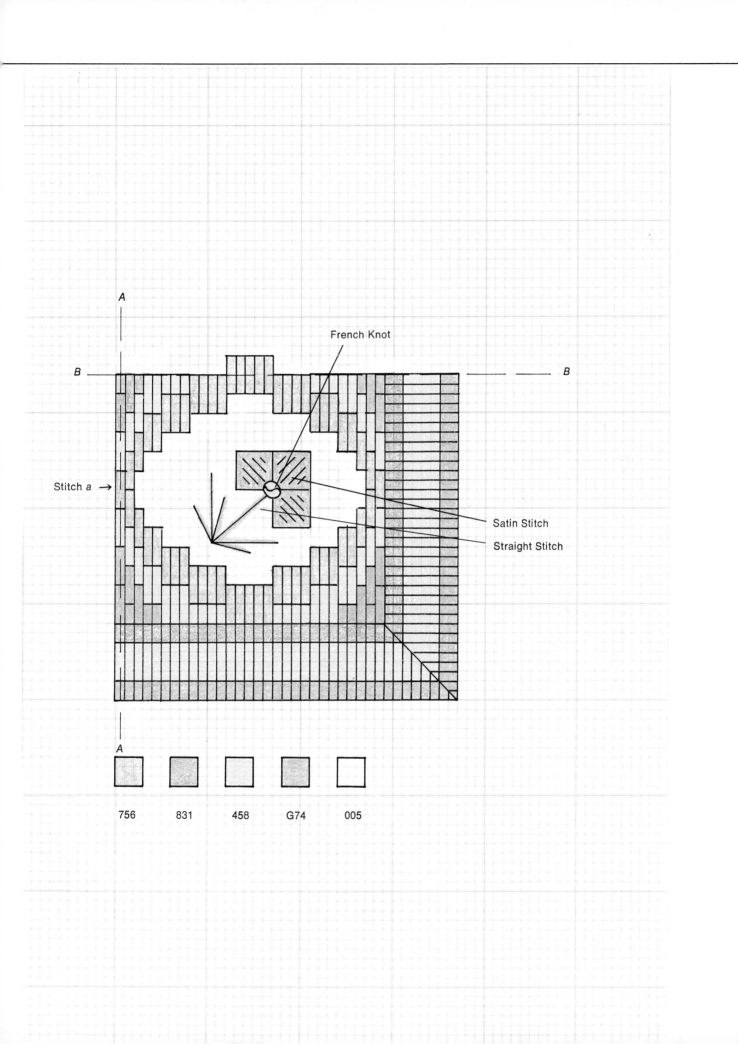

PASTEL SQUARE

the lines and place Stitch *a* on the vertical line, with the top of the stitch in the 10th mesh. Count the blue Bargello outline, noting that the five stitches at the top of the oval motif extend 2 mesh across the horizontal line. These stitches are shared with the motif in the section above.

Place the blue outlines in all four sections. Work the center motif openings in Basket Weave Stitch. Fill in the corners and center diamond with Bargello, using the colors shown. Outline the square with 3 rows of Gobelin Stitch in the colors and widths indicated on the chart to form a border. With a single strand of matching yarn, work a row of Back Stitch between the Gobelin rows.

Using two-ply yarn, work the embroidery motifs on top of the needlepoint as shown. Slant the Satin Stitch in the petals in the direction shown by the diagonal lines on the flower. Place a French Knot at the join of the three petals. Leaves and stem are Straight Stitches placed as on the drawing.

To make into the pillow shown, construct as follows:

Cut two 13″ squares of the white fabric. Block the needlepoint and trim the canvas borders to ½″. Turn these edges to wrong side and steam. Center the square on one of the pieces of fabric and sew it with small invisible stitches. Steam.

Lay the second piece of fabric on a flat surface, right side up. Place the piece with the needlepoint attached on top with the wrong side up, lining up the edges carefully. Top with the layer of quilt batting. Pin the three layers together and stitch along the edges of all four sides, leaving a 6″ opening at the bottom. Trim corners and cut excess batting from seam. Turn. Press.

Measure in from the outside edges 1½″ and place a row of machine stitching around the pillow, leaving at least a 5″ opening at the bottom to receive the stuffing. Stuff lightly. Machine-stitch the opening carefully to complete the row of stitching that forms the tuck. Turn the edges of the remaining opening at the outside to the inside and slipstitch closed.

The green cord at the inside of the tucked "cuff" is a three-ply strand of Persian yarn couched over the machine stitching.

EMBROIDERY ON FABRIC

EMBROIDERY ON FABRIC

The group of designs in this section comprises embroidery on a fabric background rather than the canvas of the previous section. The stitches are the same, but working methods differ somewhat and the finished products are vastly different in appearance. There are crewel designs worked in the traditional wool yarns, counted Cross Stitch, a Bargello design to work on velveteen, and embroidery in lustrous cotton floss. The collection itself is just a sampling of the many kinds of fabric embroidery to be found, but hopefully all the items are interesting and useful.

TRANSFERRING THE DESIGNS TO FABRIC

Line drawings of the exact size of the embroideries are provided for every project, so there will be no enlarging problems for those who cannot draw. Trace them with one of the new hot-iron transfer or copy pencils and transfer them from the tissue paper without recopying. Note that the designs appear in this book in reverse position so that when transferred directly in the manner described, the pattern will be exactly like the finished model.

To join the sections of large designs that have been divided across two (or more) pages, trace them onto parchment that has been folded in half (or into quarters), matching the fold lines of the paper to the dashed lines on the drawings. It is usually best to trace all the sections on the parchment, check to make certain that all are placed properly, then go over the outlines with the transfer pencil in preparation to ironing the design onto the fabric.

When tracing for the transfer, work with a very sharp pencil to keep the lines fine. If a mistake is made, begin over with a new sheet of paper, as the error will transfer to the fabric and may be in an area that will not be covered with embroidery. Move the iron over the transfer pattern carefully to avoid displacing it or smearing the lines. Make a small practice tracing and transfer it to a corner of the fabric to check iron temperature as well as visibility of the color pencil on the fabric. Pencils are available in both blue and magenta in most needlework supply stores at a very moderate price.

IDENTIFICATION OF YARNS AND STITCHES ON CHARTS

Lowercase letters (a, b, etc.) on each chart indicate the stitches used on the model, while numbers identify the yarn or floss colors. As in the preceding section, threads are identified by the manufacturer's color numbers and color names (where applicable) to simplify shopping for materials. All Persian yarn numbers are for either Columbia-Minerva Needlepoint and Crewel Yarn or the equally familiar Paternayan Persian. In a few cases the color is available only in the Paternayan brand and this is noted by an asterisk (*) after the color number. The two yarns can be mixed with no problem, as both are fine-quality wool with the same color standards.

MATERIALS AND TECHNIQUES

Yarn Requirements

When yarn requirements are noted in skein quantities, these are based on Columbia-Minerva's 25-yard pull skein. When yarn quantities are stated in yards, these estimates are based on three-ply strands. Naturally, yarns other than those listed may be substituted if colors match, but care should be taken to compare skein yardages so correct amounts can be purchased.

Embroidery floss numbers are for DMC six-strand cotton embroidery floss, which is sold in 8-yard skeins. Other brands may be substituted if the colors are available.

The yardage suggested for each color in the list of materials for each project is based on requirements for the finished model shown. The quantity should be adequate for the average careful worker to finish the project with a small unavoidable surplus. The working methods used to determine these estimates were normal ones, with no special emphasis on conserving yarn, but no material was wasted. If you know you are extravagant with yarn or if you decide to change stitches or enlarge the design, please add to the suggested yardages to avoid disappointment.

Fabrics

Enough time is invested in every piece of embroidery to make it important that only high-quality materials be used. It is impossible to identify the manufacturers of all the background fabrics used in the projects, but it is not difficult to find appropriate substitutes in the stores. The instructions for each model describe the fabric briefly to make purchase of a similar product possible. Most of the natural-colored linen shown is Belgian of a fine quality, heavy and regular in weave. The colored linens are dress fabrics. All the accessories used to complete the projects are readily available in fabric or needlework shops.

Frames and Hoops

It is best to work most embroidery on fabric with the fabric stretched in a hoop or frame. The variety of these is great, and selection can be based on personal preference as well as on price. Hand-held hoops are fine for small pieces, but generally a large piece is best worked on a roller frame or one of the self-supporting hoops that leaves both hands free to work. Embroidering on a frame takes a short adjustment while learning to stitch with one hand above and one hand below the work, but speed is so quickly gained and the results are so beautiful that it is difficult to go back to the hand-held hoop.

Needles

Choose embroidery needles carefully. They should be the familiar long-eyed crewel type, and the size should be suitable to both the fabric and the yarn to be used. Ideally, the needle should pierce the fabric easily, making an opening just large enough for the yarn to pass through without too much friction.

Find the best-quality needles available, as less expensive ones corrode quickly and are difficult to use.

Threading the Needle

Never wet or twist the yarn to thread the needle. Either use the methods illustrated in the diagrams on page 15 or use one of the small-metal needle threaders.

Length of Yarn or Thread

Work with short threads. Normally, crewel yarn lengths should not be more than 18"; otherwise, it wears thin and does not cover well. Embroidery floss tangles and knots if it is too long, so keep it short also.

Avoiding Knots

Learn to embroider without knots. This is not the impossible task it seems. Begin stitching on the right side with several running stitches in an area that will be covered with embroidery. Leave the end on the right side and clip it off when it is reached. Fasten the end of a strand in the same manner. This method avoids knots, saves the time that would be spent turning the frame over to fasten ends, and eliminates loose yarn ends hanging on the back of the embroidery. The wrong side will never be as beautiful as the right, but at least it can be as neat as possible.

Thinning or Breaking of Yarn

If wool yarn wears thin, even when a short length is being used, check the needle. It may be a size too small, causing too much wear on the yarn as it is being pulled through the fabric. Some needles also have eyes shaped in such a way that they cut the yarn if too much pulling takes place. Keep an assortment of needles on hand and change until the right one is found.

Working with the Twist of the Yarn

Each strand of wool yarn is made up of hundreds of short fibers spun into a continuous thread. If the strand is pulled through the thumb and forefinger, the "grain" or spinning direction can be felt. Pulled in one direction the thread is smooth, while the short fiber ends can be felt if the direction is reversed. The yarn should always be threaded into the needle so the smooth side follows the needle into the fabric. This reduces abrasion and

wear on the yarn and produces smoother embroidery.

Sorting Yarn

Sort yarns in daylight and mark them with color numbers to correspond to the ones on the charts. Many embroiderers like to keep yarn colors separated in plastic sandwich bags with color numbers marked on them. New devices to make sorting and marking easier include lucite pallets, fancy caddies, and a fascinatingly simple plastic slotted ruler-type sorter that had to be designed by an embroiderer genius. It is a slightly flexible plastic strip with numbered slots for twenty shades of yarn and also includes a 6" ruler on one edge. The price is so small, the idea so ingenious, and the device so useful that it quickly becomes a workbasket necessity.

Thimbles

Use a thimble if you are in the habit of using it for other sewing, but do not fret if you find it more trouble than it is worth. Beautiful embroidery can be worked with or without a thimble, but good scissors and adequate light are absolutely essential.

Covering Transfer Lines

Embroider slightly beyond the outlines of the design on the fabric to be certain the color from the transfer is completely covered. Work stitches with a slightly loose tension to allow the yarn to "relax" a little and to provide good coverage, especially in stitches worked solid to cover an area.

COUNTED CROSS STITCH

Counted Cross Stitch is an engrossing embroidery that has a beautiful nostalgic appeal. Worked on an even-weave fabric, the stitches are identical in size and always in perfect alignment. The embroidery is so much more beautiful than that worked on stamped crosses that it is impossible to accept the irregularity of stamped work once the Counted Cross is attempted.

Choose good-quality Hardanger, Aidia, or even-weave linen with a thread count that will produce the size stitches desired. Pull a thread across the fabric and cut on the line to cut perfectly.

The top stitch of every Cross Stitch must always slant in one direction throughout the entire piece of embroidery to assure a smooth, regular appearance. To avoid confusion about the slant of the stitches, always hold the piece in the same position (with the selvages running the same way).

When working from the counted Cross Stitch charts, note that each square indicates a stitch of a particular color worked over the prescribed number of threads. The Gardener's Sampler on page 94 is on Hardanger fabric, with each stitch worked over a square 2 threads by 2 threads. When counting unworked spaces between motifs, be sure to allow for this.

Work individual motifs rather than attempting to work across an entire row. Do not "jump" across unworked background spaces with long threads. Dark-colored threads may show through the fabric when the piece is stretched, and threads pulled too tightly will prevent the piece from being blocked flat.

Two basting threads through the center of the piece—one horizontally and one vertically—are great timesavers and help in the counting for placement of motifs. It is usually best to find an anchor point from which to start counting and work outward from that point. Some prefer to start working at the exact center of the piece, while others prefer to begin at the top corner and proceed downward. One's method should be based on individual working preferences as well as on the design itself. Either method works perfectly if it is carried through to the finish.

USING THE DESIGNS FOR ORIGINAL PROJECTS

Although the embroideries are shown developed into specific items, most are adaptable to many other uses. Stitches and colors can be changed to fit individual needs; multicolored designs can be adapted to monochromatic schemes; picture ideas can be used for pillows, book-covers, tray inserts, or stool tops; small motifs can be combined in interesting ways and, marvel of marvels, finished models can be duplicated by following the instructions! Enjoy the designs and use them in any way that suits your fancy!

CREWEL PICTURE AND PILLOW

Early American crewel-embroidered bed-covers, valances, and petticoat borders often featured scattered design motifs similar to this. The colors found on surviving embroideries vary greatly—some are bright using a myriad hues; Deerfield embroidery was done in shades of indigo; other examples blended home-dyed yarns into subtly beautiful compositions. This easy little piece is worked in six closely blended shades of rose and three soft greens on a background fabric of tightly woven white wool serge. A pretty variation could be embroidered in a multicolored selection of yarns.

A layer of polyester quilt filler was placed under the embroidery before it was stretched and placed in the frame. This gives a soft rounded look that is very attractive for crewel pictures.

The pillow back was made from the same white serge that was used for the embroidery. The pair of items made from the same design makes a nice accent for any room. Many designs can be used thus in more than one way.

Finished size: Design area: 6″ × 7″
Frame: 8″ × 10″ oval
Finished pillow: 11″ × 11″, excluding the ruffle
Materials: Fabric for either picture or pillow: 12″ square
Crewel needle
Persian yarn (three-ply), 4 yards each of the following colors: 205–Reddish Brown; 236–Burgundy; 234–Toasty Pink; 281–Antique Pink; 865–Powder Pink; 837–Whisper Pink; 528–Forest Green; 535–Fern; 537–Iced Mint
Either fabric and lace for pillow or oval 8″ × 10″ frame as shown

Note: Work all embroidery stitches with a single ply of yarn.

Instructions: Trace the drawing and transfer it to the fabric. Stretch tightly in an embroidery hoop or frame and embroider, following the chart for stitches and colors to be used. Pad all Satin and Fishbone Stitches with an outline of Back Stitch in matching color to achieve a heavy, raised look. Work the Split Stitch in rows following the outline of the shapes, placing the rows close together for a solid filling.

Block the completed embroidery and make up into a pillow or frame as shown.

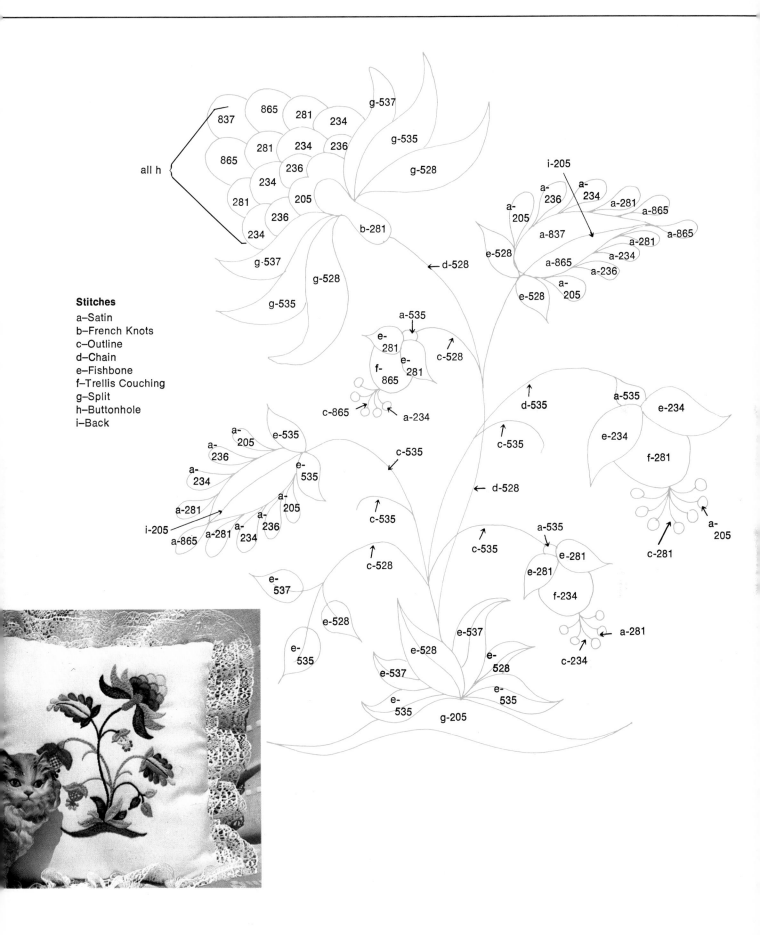

Stitches
a–Satin
b–French Knots
c–Outline
d–Chain
e–Fishbone
f–Trellis Couching
g–Split
h–Buttonhole
i–Back

all h

837
865 281 234
865 281 234 236   g-537
281 234 236   g-535
234 205   g-528
236
b-281

g-537
g-528
g-535

i-205
a-236   a-234
a-205   a-281   a-865
a-837   a-865
a-865   a-281
e-528   a-234   a-865
         a-236
e-528   a-205

d-528

a-535
e-281
e-281   c-528
f-865
c-865   a-234

c-535

d-535   a-535
c-535   e-234
           e-234
d-528   f-281

a-205
e-535
a-236   c-281
a-234   e-535
a-281   a-205   a-535
i-205   a-236   e-281
a-865 a-281 a-234   e-281
                 f-234
e-537
c-535   a-281
c-528   c-234
e-528
e-535
e-537   e-528   e-537
e-535   e-528
        g-205   e-535

CARNATION AND OAK LEAF PICTURE

The springtime freshness of this pink and green composition on a nubby white linen would be a gay accent for most any room. The size of the picture was planned so it could be made up into a matching 14″ pillow without design adjustment.

Although only a few embroidery stitches have been used, each works in its own way to accent the design. Long-and-Short delicately shades the carnations from pale pink at the outer edges of the petals to deep reddish brown at the center, while rows of Chain Stitch placed close together carry out the delicate variations of the oak leaves, and Buttonhole Stitch separates and defines the small petals of the center buds. Other stitches and colors would create an entirely different feeling, so follow instructions or try new combinations. Either way, have fun!

Finished size: Design area: 12″ × 12″
Frame size: 19″ × 19″
Mat opening: 14″ × 14″
If desired, make up into a 14″-square pillow.
Materials: Textured white linen 20″ × 20″ for picture; 15″ × 15″ sufficient for pillow
Crewel needle
Persian yarn as follows: *5 yards each:* 565–Yellow Green; 550–Antique Lime; 545–Avocado; 865–Powder Pink; 281–Antique Pink; 234–Toasty Pink; 205–Reddish Brown; *10 yards each:* 575–Spring Pea Green; 570–Celery Leaf; 555–Green Giant; 510–Medium Green; 520–Hunter Green
Finishing materials: Either frame and mat or ½ yard appropriate fabric for pillow back

Note: All yarn quantities are for three-ply yarn. Separate the yarn and work all embroidery with a single strand.

Instructions: The diagram is for one-half of the piece. Trace as follows to assure correct layout.

Fold a sheet of parchment into quarters and, matching the folds to the dashed lines in the charts on pages 82 and 83, trace both sections onto the left half of the paper. Turn the tracing paper clockwise until your copy of Carnation #1 is at the top right and the dashed lines match. Repeat the procedure to complete the other half. Transfer the design to linen.

Stretch the linen in an embroidery frame or large hoop. The numbers and letters on the chart indicate the colors and stitches that were used in the finished model. Use the detail photograph for additional help in the embroidery if needed.

Work the carnation petals in Long-and-Short, starting with the palest pink, 865, at the tips and working through 281 and 234 to the deep Reddish Brown (205) at the inside. Work heavily, placing the stitches close together or on top of each other to achieve a blended or painted effect. The scalloped section of the flower is worked in rows of Split Stitch closely spaced. The oval shapes inside that portion are Lazy Daisy with a single Straight Stitch in 565–Yellow Green as filling.

The stems of the carnations and the center buds are to be worked in Split Stitch beginning with an outline of 510–Medium Green and filling in toward the center with rows of 545, 550, and 565 in that order.

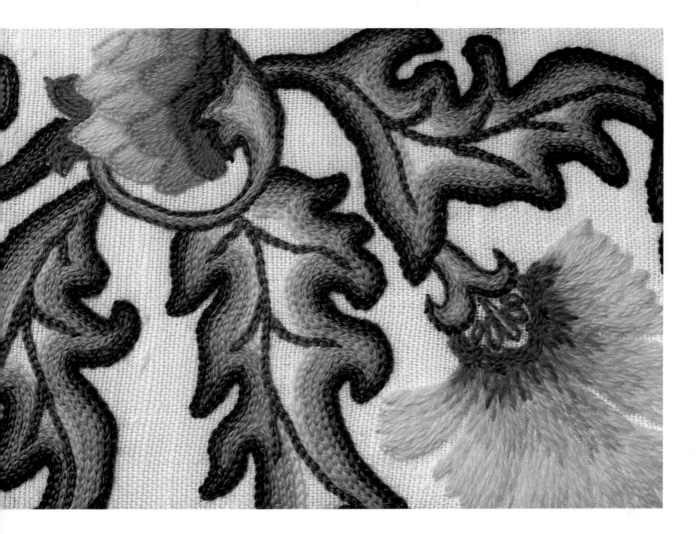

This detail from the picture shows the way rows of Chain Stitch in shades of green are used to make gracefully detailed leaves. Note that the centers of the leaves, in the colonial manner, are left unworked. Use the photograph showing the completed project (page 83) as well as the chart as an aid in working the Long-and-Short flowers and the Buttonhole Stitch buds.

CARNATION AND OAK LEAF PICTURE

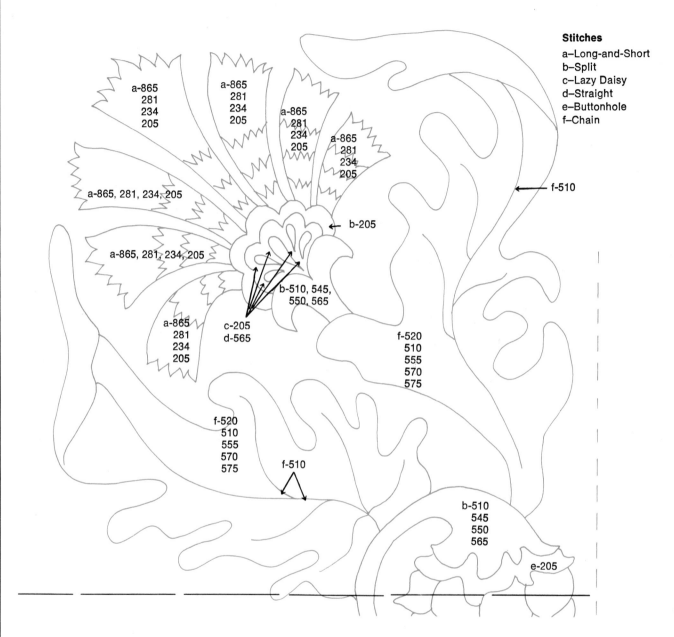

The center buds are worked in Buttonhole Stitch using the shades of pink as noted on the chart. The two small petals at the tip of each bud should be worked in rows of Split Stitch in 205–Reddish Brown.

All oak leaves are to be worked in Chain Stitch, beginning with an outline row of 520–Hunter Green. Shade the leaves from the dark outline to the lightest of the grass greens by working rows close together and using the colors in order from 510, 555, 570, and 575. Work center vein also in Chain Stitch in color 510–Medium Green. There will be small sections of linen visible in the middle of the leaves.

Block the completed embroidery and frame; or make into a pillow.

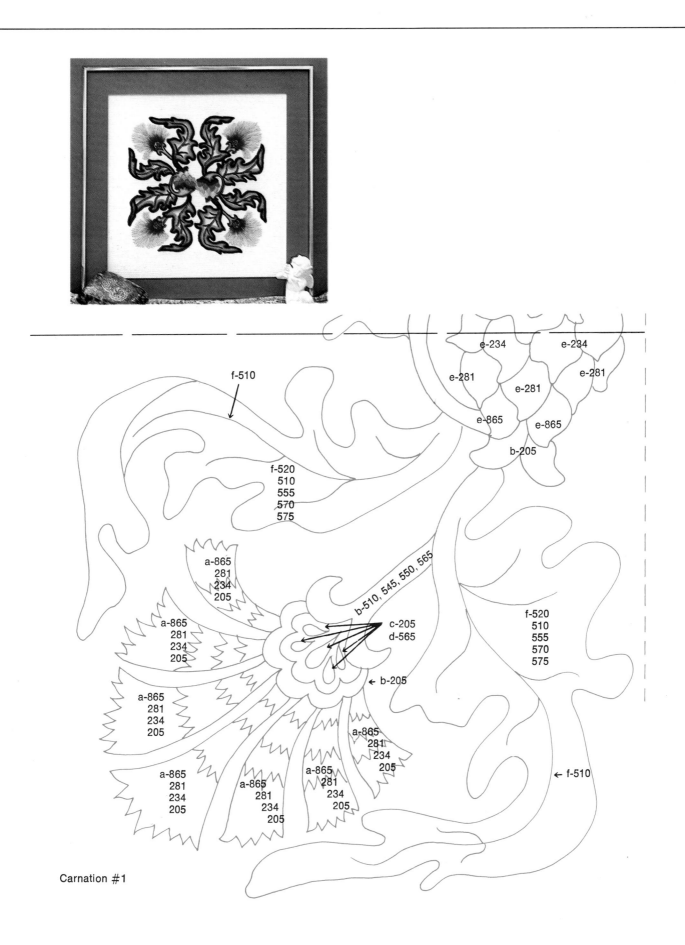

f-510

e-234   e-234

e-281   e-281

e-281

e-865   e-865

b-205

f-520
510
555
570
575

a-865
281
234
205

a-865
281
234
205

b-510, 545, 550, 565

c-205
d-565

f-520
510
555
570
575

a-865
281
234
205

← b-205

a-865
281
234
205

a-865
281
234
205

a-865
281
234
205

a-865
281
234
205

← f-510

Carnation #1

BIRD PILLOW

Reembroidered fabric is sometimes the answer to the problem of finding the perfect accessory for a room decorated with patterned fabric. The result can be a handsome customized pillow that fits perfectly into the room and adds the texture and luxury of embroidery. Many types of fabric are adaptable to this technique—prints can be floral, scenic, geometric, ethnic, and so on.

This lovely floral featuring a bird of bright plumage was an easy one to embroider—colors match the fabric as closely as possible, the design is large, and the stitches are all easy ones. Detail photographs illustrate the way the stitches were used to accent the design. Lazy Daisy was perfect for the hydrangea blossoms above the bird. Where the petal was wider than the stitch would have been naturally, an extra little Couching-like stitch holds the yarn in a rounder shape. French Knots make the flower centers.

The bird is worked predominantly in Long-and-Short Stitch, and the color blending is as close as possible to that printed on the fabric. His body is outlined with Split Stitch, while Chain and Split combine on his legs. Overlapping Lazy Daisy Stitch makes the feather outlines at the top of his wing.

The large flowers, leaves, and tree trunk are primarily Long-and-Short Stitch outlined with Split Stitch. Color shading came directly from the fabric. Clusters of French Knots are a natural for the raised flower centers.

Working in this manner on a printed fabric is a kind of adventure in stitchery. Any stitches or combinations of stitches can be used; texture can be heavy or light according to the desired finished look; colors can match or be slightly different to set the embroidery apart from the balance of the print. This is fun! It is embroidery without a kit, so there is a great deal of freedom possible, but no drawing or designing talent is required. Only after it has been attempted does one appreciate just how interesting this technique can be!

Facing page—top: A closeup of one of the flowers from the pillow shows Long-and-Short Stitches worked in colors to match the print of the fabric. The stitches are worked closely to completely cover the print and to add texture. Facing page—bottom: The use of embroidery stitches over the print gives the bird texture and importance, while the print underneath acts as a very good pattern. Other details from this pillow appear among the embroidery stitch illustrations at the back of the book.

CREWEL PINCUSHION

Need an easy, thoughtful, feminine remembrance? This quick little pincushion trimmed with a lavish lace ruffle could be the answer—a gift that will be received with enthusiasm. Fill with dried roses for a sachet or with polyester fiber filling to use as the pincushion shown.

Finished size: 4" diameter (without lace ruffle)

Materials: Natural linen approximately 5" × 10"

Cotton lace: ½ yard in a natural or off-white color

Crewel needle

Persian yarn as follows: 385–French Blue, 2 yards; 756–Summer Blue, 2 yards; 395–Light Blue, 2 yards; 456–Baby Yellow, 1 yard; 555–Green Giant, 1 yard; 975–Pumpkin Seed, 1 yard

Small amount fiberfill

Note: Work all embroidery with a single ply of the yarn.

Instructions: Trace the design and transfer it to the linen, centering it on one-half of the piece of fabric.

Outline center flower with Split Stitch in palest shade of blue before working the Long-and-Short. Work the flower petals, shading from the pale blue at the center to French Blue at the outside edges, blending the three into each other to create a gradual change at the dashed lines.

The small yellow flowers are five Lazy Daisy Stitches with a French Knot center and a Straight Stitch of blue filling the center of each petal. Groups of leaves are also Lazy Daisy in green, with a Straight Stitch of orange filling the opening.

Steam the completed embroidery. Trim excess linen, leaving a ½" seam allowance beyond marked stitching line. Use the piece as a pattern to cut the back section from the remaining linen. Gather lace and stitch it to the linen on the stitching line. Stitch front to back, leaving a small opening. Trim seam allowance and turn right side out. Stuff lightly and close with invisible stitches.

Stitches
a–Lazy Daisy
b–French Knots
c–Long-and-Short
d–Straight

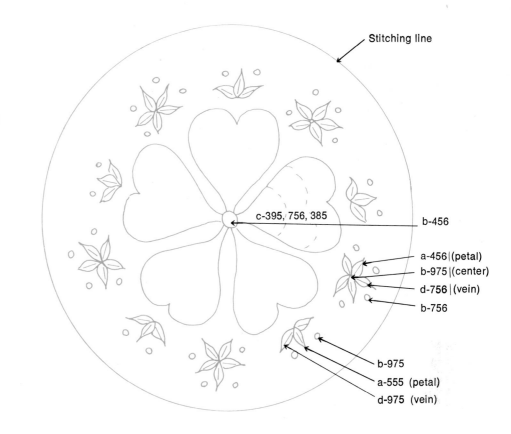

c-395, 756, 385

b-456

a-456 | (petal)
b-975 | (center)
d-756 | (vein)
b-756

b-975
a-555 (petal)
d-975 (vein)

EMBROIDERY SCISSORS CASE

Good scissors are necessary to fine embroidery, but those sharp points can be a problem in the sewing basket or carryall. This little linen case fittingly embroidered with a Jacobean flower protects both the scissors and the needlepoint. This is both a useful and pretty sewing accessory.

Finished size: 3" × 4"
Materials: Natural-colored linen approximately 10" × 12"
Polyester quilt batting approximately 4" × 10"
Embroidery needle
DMC Embroidery Floss, 1 skein each: 351–coral; 352–medium coral; 353–light coral; 445–yellow; 746–cream; 469–avocado (color names are approximate, not official)
Note: Separate the floss and work all stitches with three strands.

Instructions: Trace the embroidery design and the stitching line and transfer it to the linen, positioning it so there will be space to cut four pieces with seam allowances ½" beyond the stitching line shown on the drawing.

Embroider the front, following the chart for color placement and stitches. The dual numbers for the areas to be worked in Trellis Couching (for example, 353/351) indicate that the thread to be laid is of the first color number while the tiedown stitches are of the second color.

After all embroidery is completed, cut out the front, allowing ½" seam allowances beyond the stitching line on all sides. Using the front as a pattern, cut three more pieces for back and lining. Cut two pieces quilt batting without seam allowances. Using one of the hot-iron adhesives and applying the iron to the linen side, bond the batting to two of the unembroidered linen pieces.

With the right sides together, stitch the front to one of the padded sections, leaving most of one long side open for turning. Trim seam to ⅛" and turn right side out. Whip seam closed with invisible stitches. Repeat to make the back of case.

Embroider the row of Blanket Stitch across the top of both front and back sections. With right sides out, whip the two pieces together, keeping stitches small and closely spaced.

For the corded trim, cut a 1-yard piece of green embroidery floss. Fold it in half and, with the index finger in the fold, twist it tightly. Without releasing either end, fold the twisted thread in half again and allow it to twist back on itself. Tie the loose ends in a knot.

Using a single strand of matching thread, whip the twisted cord in place over the seam of the case, fastening the ends inside where they will not be seen.

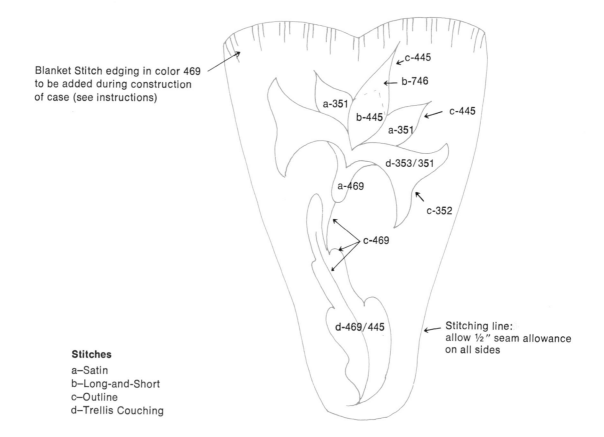

Blanket Stitch edging in color 469 to be added during construction of case (see instructions)

c-445

b-746

a-351

b-445

c-445

a-351

d-353/351

a-469

c-352

c-469

d-469/445

Stitching line: allow ½″ seam allowance on all sides

Stitches

a–Satin
b–Long-and-Short
c–Outline
d–Trellis Couching

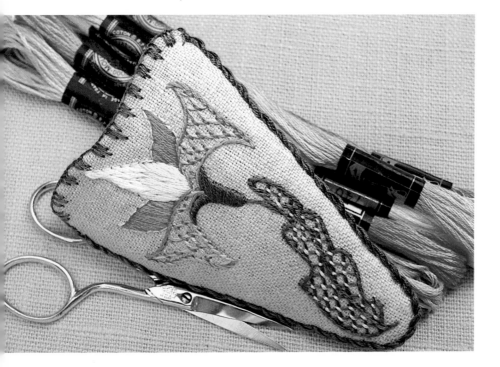

PENNSYLVANIA DUTCH BIRTH OR WEDDING SAMPLER

In the eighteenth and nineteenth centuries in that beautiful little section of Pennsylvania known as the Dutch Country, it was the custom to record births, baptisms, weddings, and deaths with a kind of illuminated manuscript called Fractur. The documents were elaborately and colorfully decorated, recorded the pertinent geneological information, and usually included several religious verses.

The Boyles family cherishes a lovely example of this folk art recording the baptism of Mr. Boyles' great-great-grandmother on June 3, 1805, in Cocalico Township of Lancaster County, Pennsylvania. When our grandson, Justin, was born, I decided to embroider a modern version of the Taufschein for him. The layout is reminiscent of the old manuscript adopting the heart as an enclosure for the written data and leaving a wide border to be decorated with flowers and birds in typically primitive Pennsylvania Dutch colors.

This was planned as the beginning of a family tradition with each grandchild receiving an adaptation of a Taufschein of his or her own. The designs would be appropriate as wedding mementoes also, and these would be correctly called Trauschein.

Finished size: Embroidery area: 11" × 13"
Frame: 13" × 17"
Materials: Linen 20" × 22"
Embroidery needle
DMC Embroidery Floss, 1 skein each:
    472–pale yellow-green; 471–light yellow-green; 3346–dark avocado; 895–forest green; 746–cream; 445–yellow; 726–bright yellow; 741–orange; 352–medium coral; 350–deep coral; 999–scarlet; 3325–rose; 813–medium blue; 322–skipper blue; 311–French blue

Instructions: With a regular pencil trace the half of design shown on the charts on pages 92 and 93 using the dashed lines as guides to matching sections; then fold the paper in half on the vertical dashed line and trace your tracing to complete the design (except for the center flower, which is already complete). Open and go over the drawing with a transfer pencil. Plan the lettering to be used and copy it inside the heart. Script most closely emulates the old-style calligraphy, but other styles will be attractive if well executed. Go over the design and lettering with a transfer pencil and transfer to the linen with a hot iron.

Letters on the chart indicate the stitches used; numbers specify colors. The dual numbers for the areas to be worked in Trellis Couching (for example, 350/726) indicate that the thread to be laid down is of the first color number while the tiedown stitches are of the second color. All stitches are worked with three strands of floss except for the Outline Stitches around motifs, which are done with a single strand. Satin Stitch should be padded with a row of Back Stitches outlining the motif. Work letters in small Back Stitches.

Block the completed embroidery according to the directions on page 154.

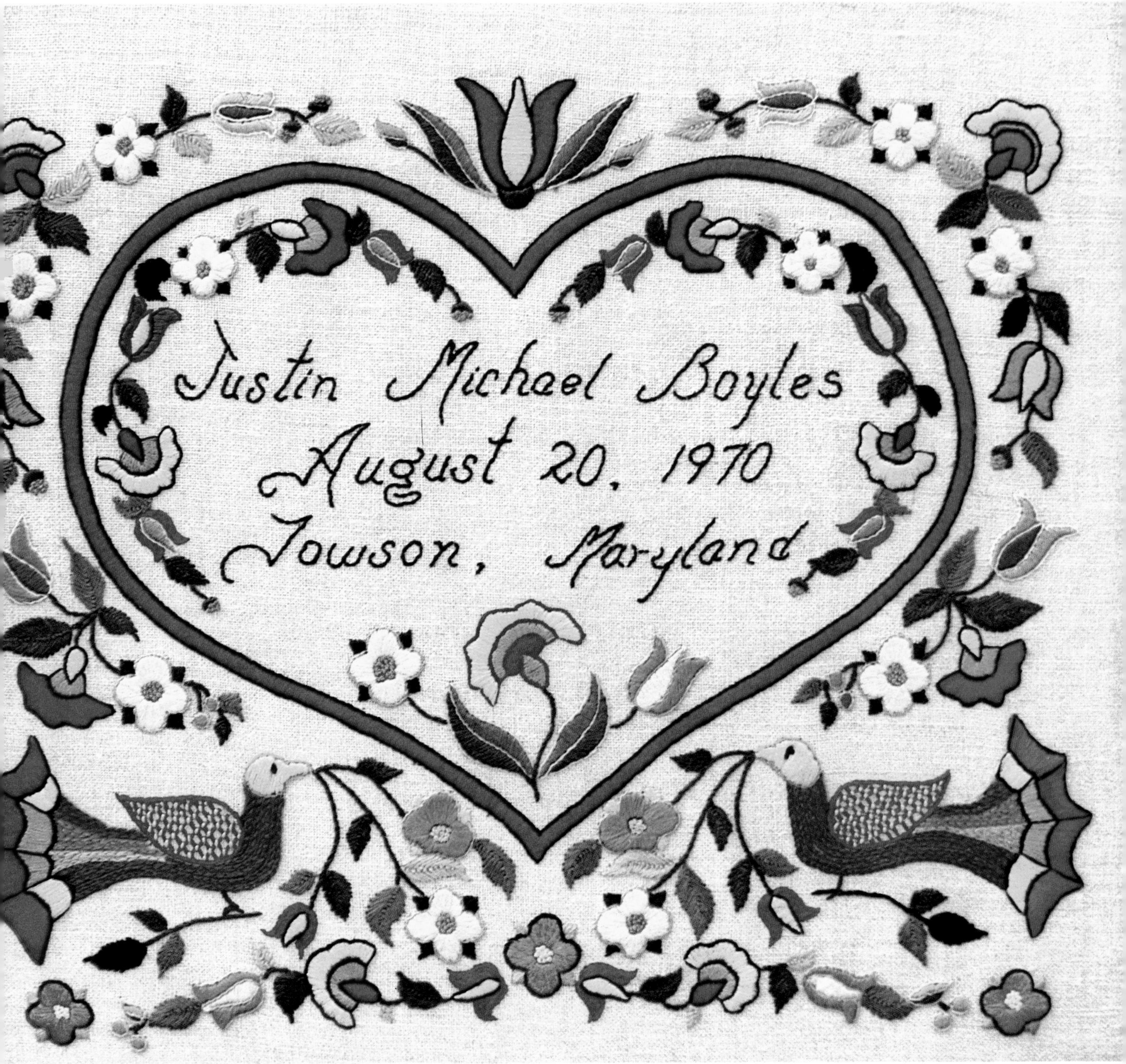
Justin Michael Boyles
August 20, 1970
Towson, Maryland

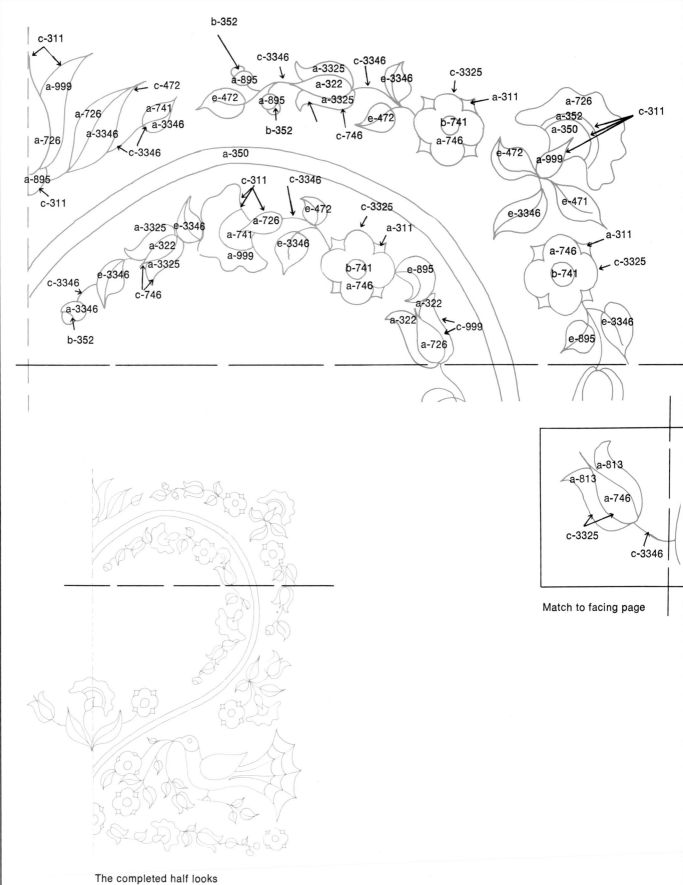

c-311

a-999

a-726

c-472

a-726

a-741

a-3346

a-3346

c-3346

a-895

c-311

b-352

a-895

e-472

a-895

b-352

c-3346

a-3325

a-322

a-3325

c-746

c-3346

e-3346

e-472

c-3325

a-311

b-741

a-746

a-726

a-352

a-350

a-999

c-311

e-472

e-471

e-3346

a-311

a-746

b-741

c-3325

a-350

c-311

c-3346

a-726

e-472

a-741

e-3346

a-999

c-3325

a-311

b-741

a-746

e-895

a-3325

e-3346

a-322

a-3325

a-3346

e-3346

a-746

c-746

c-3346

a-3346

b-352

a-322

a-322

c-999

a-726

e-3346

e-895

a-813

a-813

a-746

c-3325

c-3346

Match to facing page

The completed half looks
like this (see instructions)

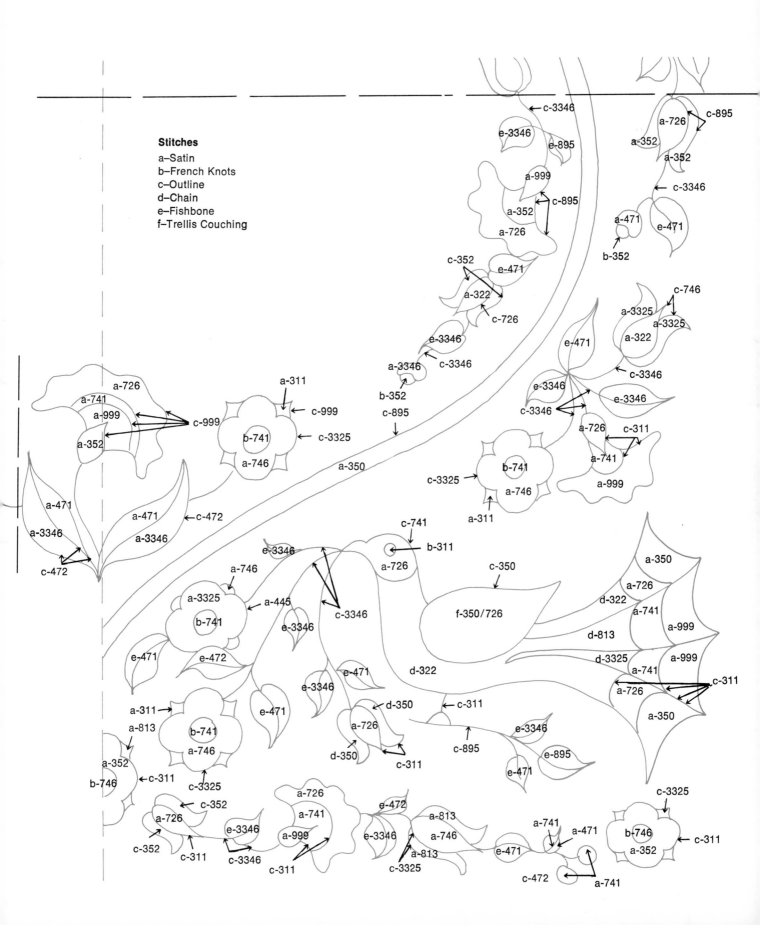

Stitches
a–Satin
b–French Knots
c–Outline
d–Chain
e–Fishbone
f–Trellis Couching

GARDENER SAMPLER

Schoolgirls of days gone by learned discipline, symmetry, stitches, and the rudiments of design on samplers not much different from this nostalgic piece. Mottoes on old samplers often included Bible quotations or inspirational verse. The quotation on this one is a humorous note in contrast to the traditional design layout and adaptations of historic motifs. The carnation or pink which appears repeatedly on old samplers is used in four variations on this piece. There are also gardeners of both sexes as well as birds, a fountain, trees, and interesting pots of flowers. The background fabric is a creamy white Hardanger fabric, which makes counting easy, and the colors are blended shades of pink, blue, gold, and green.

Below: The fountain from the center of the sampler illustrates the simplicity of the individual motifs that are combined to make this attractive hanging.

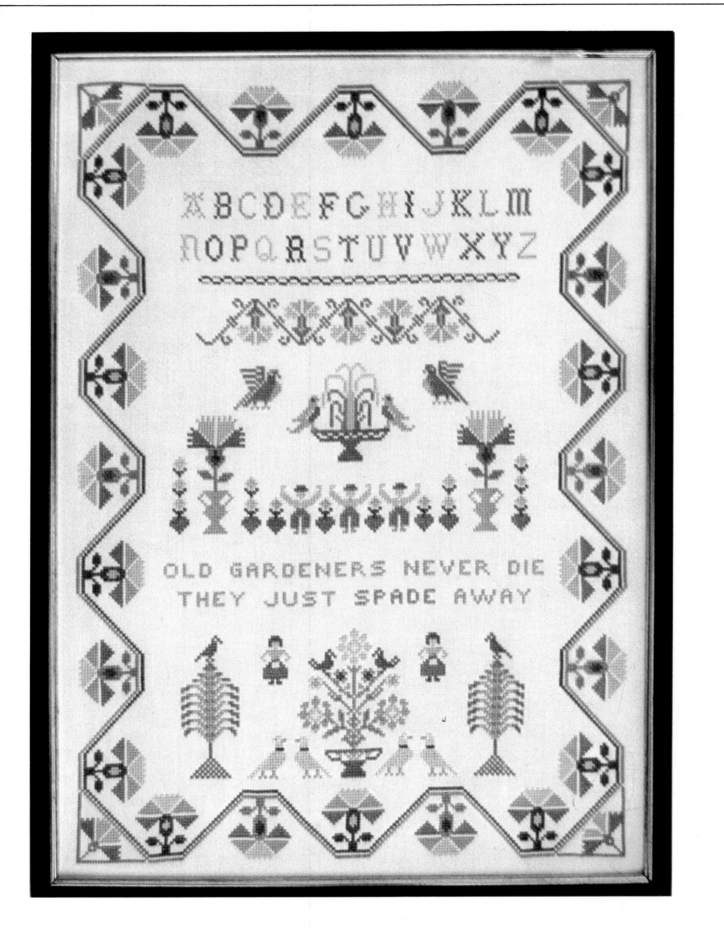

top ↑

Carnation motif
to be worked
in these spaces
throughout

Vertical center line

Horizontal center line

Chart #1

Horizontal center line

RS NEVER DIE
SPADE AWAY

Vertical center line

3328	761	754	732	728

470	471	472	445	932	775

Chart #2

GARDENER SAMPLER

To adapt the sampler for use as a birth, baptism, or wedding record, substitute the personal data for either the alphabet or the quotation or both if necessary.

Finished size: Frame opening is 18½″ × 24½″

Materials: Cream color Hardanger fabric with 22 threads to the inch; cut size no less than 23″ × 29″ to allow fabric to be laced into frame

Embroidery needles

DMC Embroidery Floss as follows: *3 skeins each:* 3328–deep pink; 761–pink; 754–pale pink; 470–medium yellow-green; 471–light yellow-green; *1 skein each:* 472–pale yellow-green; 932–pale blue; 775–baby blue; 732–antique gold; 728–pale yellow; 445–yellow

Frame as shown

Note 1: Separate the embroidery floss and work Cross Stitch with three strands throughout.

Note 2: Each colored square on the chart indicates one Cross Stitch worked over 2 horizontal and 2 vertical threads. Each white square also indicates 2 horizontal and 2 vertical threads and should be counted as such to insure proper layout.

Instructions: To prevent fraying, run a row of machine stitching—the zigzag stitch is good—around the cut edges of the fabric. Working carefully along a thread, place a basting thread through the center of the fabric both horizontally and vertically.

The design is charted in four sections. The marked horizontal and vertical center lines on the charts correspond to the bastings on the fabric. To make plain the transition from one chart to the next, there is an overlapping of key design elements. Note that at the bottom of Chart #1 only the top of the large carnation appears, while the entire motif is charted at the top of Chart #2. The same repeat effect is used for the left section of the alphabet (Chart #3) and the gardener motto (Chart #4). Use these duplicated motifs and the marked center lines to orient the charts to each other.

The carnation in the border is diagrammed in detail for the top and corner in Chart #1. The flowers are to be repeated as diagrammed in each "V" of the green trellis.

It is easiest to begin working at the top center of the border at a point 4″ down from the cut edge of the fabric (the top of Line *A* in Chart #1). Always work out from the vertical basting thread to center the rows of motifs. For smooth stitches work all Cross Stitch in the same sequence.

Block and frame as shown.

Vertical center line

Chart #3

Vertical center line

Chart #4

Facing page: Enlargement of one of the carnation borders from the sampler shows the smoothness of Cross Stitch counted on Hardanger fabric. The detail photograph in the embroidery stitch section at the back of the book shows an enlargement of one of the other carnation borders from this piece.

BARGELLO ON VELVETEEN

The use of waste canvas makes it possible to work a Four-way Bargello design on a rich velveteen background to create an elegant and unusual pillow. The stitches are worked through both canvas and velveteen, and when the canvas is removed the wool Bargello pattern is silhouetted against the lustrous velveteen background. The use of fabric as a part of the overall design eliminates many stitches, for all background work is skipped.

The Four-way design can also be used for a needlepoint pillow by working it on canvas and using either Tent or Brick Stitch to fill in the background. With a flat Tent Stitch background, the overall appearance of the pillow will be much like the pictured pillow. Brick Stitch will be faster to work and will add a slight texture to the background.

Finished size: 14″ × 14″
Materials: Waste canvas (white with blue threads to aid in counting): 18″ × 18″, 12 mesh to the inch
Royal blue cotton velveteen: 1 yard
#22 tapestry needle
Persian yarn, 1 skein each: 754–Light Medium Blue; 756–Summer Blue; 642–Bright Purple; 652–Lilac; 827– Cerise; 828–Mexican Pink
Note: Separate the yarn and work with two-ply throughout.

Instructions: Mark the waste canvas as for Four-way Bargello. From the velveteen cut one square 18″ × 18″. Lay the velveteen on a flat surface with the right side up and position the marked waste canvas on top. Match the edges and baste the two layers together. Fasten into a roller-type stretcher frame and tighten the rollers.

Work the Bargello pattern through both layers, treating them as if they were just one. Pull the stitches slightly tighter than for Bargello on canvas, as they will be looser after the canvas has been removed from under them. If it is difficult to pull the needle through the velveteen, change to a smaller needle and use a needle threader if necessary.

Begin working the Bargello at the center of the canvas with Stitch *a* and work all of the light blue outlines within the quarter before beginning to fill in the colors. Complete all Bargello in the four sections.

Remove the embroidery from the frame. Unravel the canvas thread by thread, taking care not to disturb the stitches or damage the velveteen. Cut the canvas into sections and remove it a small portion at a time if it seems easier. This sounds like a long and complicated procedure, but it is actually not bad, as the waste canvas is specifically woven to make unraveling easy. Tweezers may help if they are handy.

Steam. Trim the embroidered velveteen to 15″ × 15″ and make into a pillow, using the remainder of the yard of fabric to make back and self-piping.

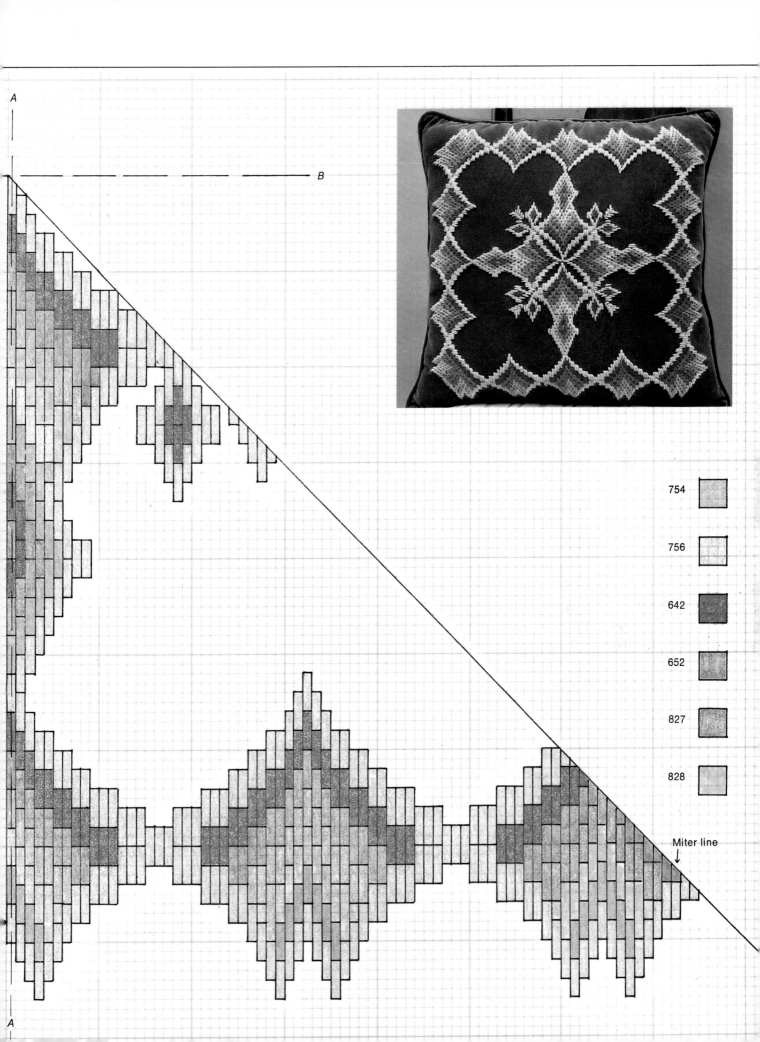

A

B

754

756

642

652

827

828

Miter line

A

EMBROIDERED MINIATURES

The luster of cotton embroidery floss highlights typical eighteenth-century crewel designs worked on a finely woven muslin background. Small designs like this are often prettier in the fine stitches of cotton thread than in the heavy wool yarns so often associated with these traditional florals.

Finished size: 4" × 5" oval
Materials: Muslin approximately 10" × 17"
#8 embroidery needle
DMC Embroidery Floss, 1 skein each:
351–coral; 352–medium coral; 353–light coral; 931–old blue; 932–pale blue; 775–baby blue; 469–avocado; 470–medium yellow-green; 725–gold
Pair of oval frames 4" × 5", as shown
Note: Separate the floss and work all stitches with three strands.

Instructions: Trace the drawings and transfer to muslin. Embroider with the stitches and colors noted on the diagrams. When Satin Stitch is used, pad it with a row of Split Stitch outlining the shape. The "holddown" threads for all Trellis Couching are yellow.

Steam the completed embroidery and frame.

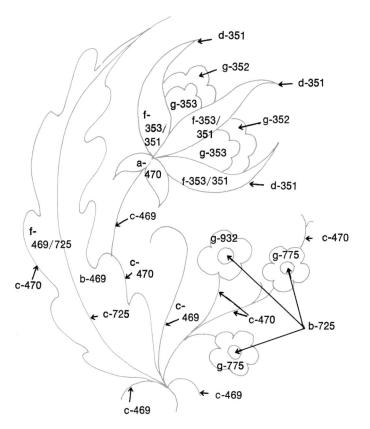

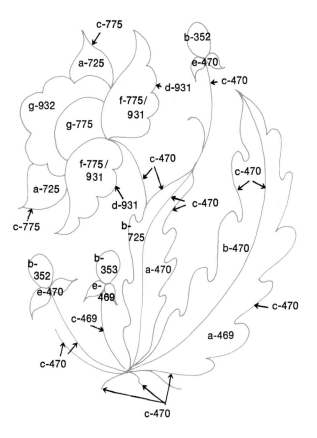

Stitches

a–Satin
b–French Knots
c–Outline
d–Chain
e–Fishbone
f–Trellis Couching
g–Buttonhole

CREWEL PURSE

This summer handbag of practical muslin is brightened with a spray of crewel flowers in the gayest colors of the season. The stitches are easy, the wool embroidery is finished quickly, and the wood frame is readily detached, so you can make several in different colors.

The wooden "bag sticks" are sold ready to be painted, stained, or waxed (as was this pair). The fabric handle can be adjusted to any length. The major pattern companies sell patterns for bags similar to this on which the embroidery design can also be used. Naturally their sewing guides are very complete, but the bag is so easy many can make it following the cutting and stitching instructions below.

Finished size: 12″ × 9″ × 2″
Materials: Heavy muslin or linen: ½ yard, 45″ wide
Fabric for lining: ½ yard
Crewel needles
Persian yarn, 5 yards each (except where noted): 855–Peony; 860–Magnolia; 865–Powder Pink; 754–Light Medium Blue; 756–Summer Blue; 395–Light Blue; 427–Medium Gold; 440–Topaz; 456–Baby Yellow; *510–Medium Green, 8 yards*; 545–Avocado; 550–Antique Lime; 565–Yellow Green
One pair wooden "bag sticks"
Note: Work all embroidery with a single ply of the Persian yarn.

Instructions: Using the dimensions on the cutting diagram cut two pieces for the bag and two for the lining. Trim the remaining strip across the width of the fabric to 3″ × 42″ for the strap.

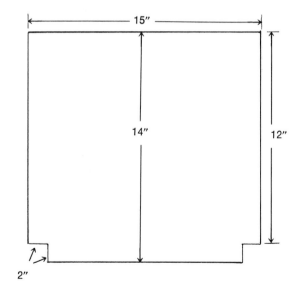

CREWEL PURSE

Trace the embroidery drawing and transfer it to the front of the bag, placing the bottom of the design 3" from the lower edge of the fabric.

Embroider, following the chart for stitches and color placement. Use the photographs also as an aid in the embroidery. Note that the Trellis Couching on the large central flower is held in place by small Cross Stitches, while on the leaves a single Straight Stitch holds the threads. The laid threads are to be in the first color noted, while the tiedown threads are of the second color. The flowers worked in Long-and-Short shade from pale at the outside edges to deep at the center. Shade the six petals of the pink flower at the upper right so they seem to stand apart. Pad all Satin Stitch areas with an outline of Split Stitch.

Steam or block the finished embroidery. Make darts at the bottom of the bag by bringing together the edges of the 2" cutouts and making a ⅝" seam. Join front to back of the bag, leaving a 6" opening at the top of each side seam. Make lining in the same manner and insert it into the bag. Turn seam allowances of the openings at the top sides of the bag and lining to inside and whip together. Turn the top edges of the bag to inside to form a 1½" casing for rods.

Fold the raw edges of the strap to inside and stitch. Insert the wooden rods into the casing and thread the strap through the slots in the rods. Tie ends.

To help with the embroidery this enlargement shows just one of the flowers on the purse. Shading and stitch direction are apparent and are more easily followed than written instructions.

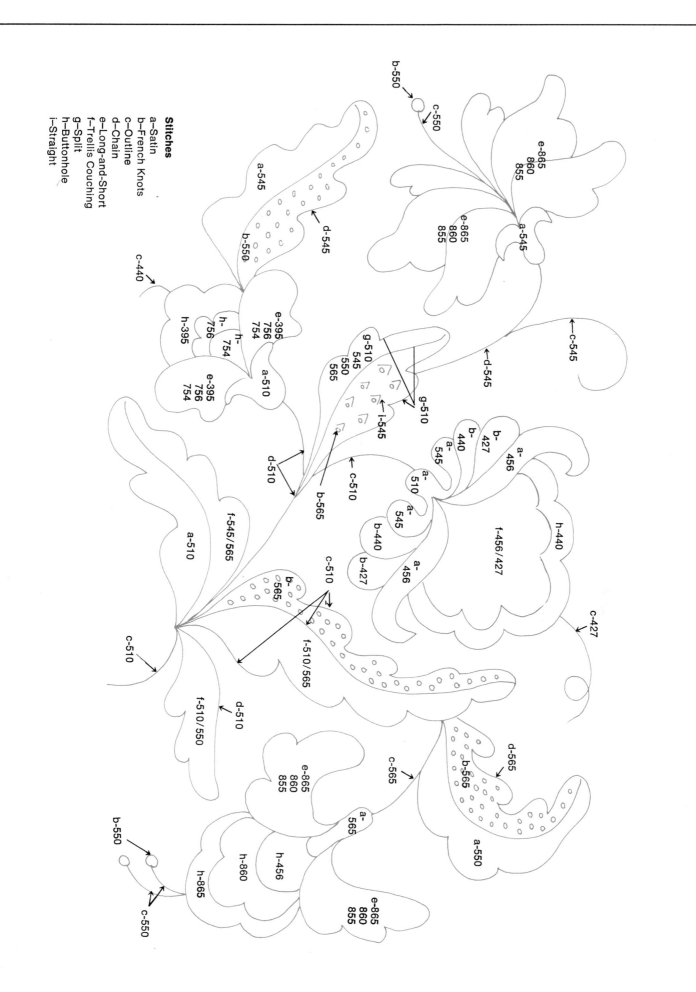

Stitches

a—Satin
b—French Knots
c—Outline
d—Chain
e—Long-and-Short
f—Trellis Couching
g—Split
h—Buttonhole
i—Straight

b-550

c-550

e-865
860
855

e-865
860
855

a-545

a-545

d-545

b-550

c-440

c-545

d-545

e-395
756
754

h-
756
754

h-395

h-

g-510
545
550
565

g-510

a-510

i-545

e-395
756
754

d-510

d-510

b-565

c-510

b-
427

b-
440

a-
545

a-
456

a-
510

a-
545

b-440

b-427

a-
456

f-456/427

h-440

c-427

f-545/565

a-510

c-510

b-
565

c-510

f-510/565

c-510

f-510/550

d-510

c-565

d-565

b-565

a-
565

a-550

e-865
860
855

h-456

h-860

h-865

b-550

c-550

e-865
860
855

GREEN LINEN PILLOW

Monochromatic embroidery in the beiges on a kelly green linen background makes a stylish pillow. A variety of stitches create a lot of textural interest and keep the embroidery interesting.

The design can also be worked in a bright multicolor mix on a light background for a surprisingly different look. The beiges can also be used on brown, blue, or red linen for an effect very much like the worked model.

Finished size: 14" × 14"
Materials: Kelly green linen: ½ yard
Embroidery needles
Contrasting piping if desired
Persian yarn as follows: 012–Ivory, 9
    yards; 020–Neutral, 8 yards; 138–
    Beige, 8 yards; 257–Light Tan, 8
    yards; 410–Coppertone, 8 yards;
    405–Copper, 9 yards
Note: Separate the yarn and work all
    stitches with a single ply.

Instructions: Trace the design using the dashed lines as a matching guide and tranfer to linen at least 15" square. Place in hoop and embroider, following the chart for color and stitch placement. Use the closeup photograph as an aid in the embroidery. Note also that several small portions of this pillow are shown with the stitch illustrations on pages 136, 138, and 140. These will provide additional visual help.

The strawberries are to be worked in Satin Stitch with Trellis Couching on top and finished with an outline row in the color matching the Couching. If all Fishbone Stitch leaves are first outlined with Split Stitch, they will be slightly raised. The large petals of the flower at the upper right should have the teardrop-shaped sections worked first in Satin Stitch, then the Trellis Couching worked over both the Satin and plain sections to duplicate the unusual effect. To create the flowing, shaded effect on the lower sections of the central leaf, work rows of closely spaced Split Stitch beginning with the deepest brown and working through the range to Neutral.

Complete all embroidery and block and construct the pillow using the remainder of the linen for the back.

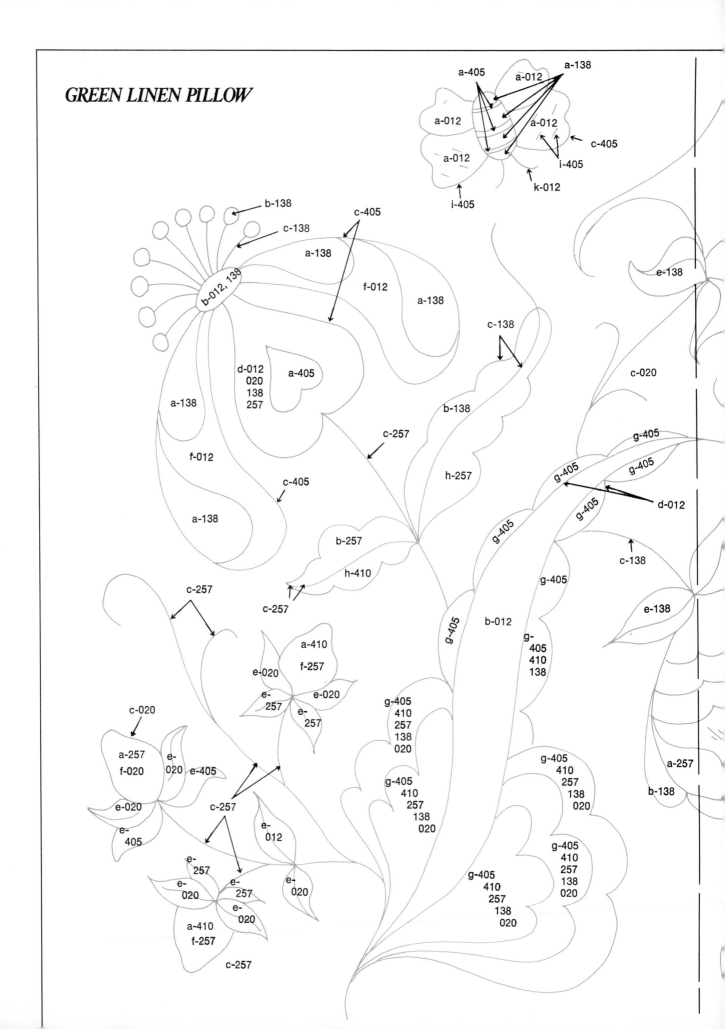

GREEN LINEN PILLOW

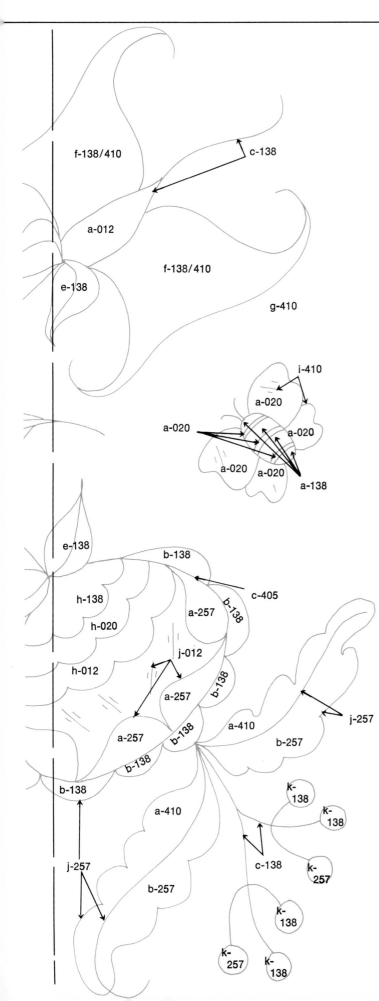

Stitches
a—Satin
b—French Knots
c—Outline
d—Chain
e—Fishbone
f—Trellis Couching
g—Split
h—Buttonhole
i—Straight
j—Back
k—Bullion Knots

f-138/410

c-138

a-012

f-138/410

e-138

g-410

i-410

a-020

a-020

a-020

a-020

a-020

a-138

e-138

b-138

h-138

c-405

a-257

b-138

h-020

j-012

h-012

a-257

b-138

a-257

a-410

j-257

a-257

b-138

b-257

b-138

b-138

k-138

b-138

k-138

a-410

c-138

k-257

j-257

k-138

b-257

k-257

k-138

WHITE-ON-WHITE DRAWSTRING POUCH

White wool embroidery in easy crewel stitches trims this old-fashioned draw-string pouch. The typically early American design motif was adapted from a carnation found on an antique pocket and may be worked on both sides of the bag for an extra luxury.

The pouch itself, an easy sewing project, can be made following the instructions here or from a purchased pattern which includes detailed sewing information and diagrams. Appropriate fabrics include wool serge, as shown in the finished model, other soft wool or wool-blend fabrics, linen, denim, satin, and crepe.

Finished size: 10½″ × 11″ (before draw-strings are pulled)
Materials: Fabric for bag: approximately 12″ × 24″
Lining fabric: approximately 12″ × 24″
Drawstrings: 1½ yards Rattail braid or Soutache cord
Crewel needle
White yarn, 005, 1 skein
Note: All embroidery should be worked with a single ply of the yarn.

Instructions: Make a tissue pattern for the bag by tracing the chart and adding ½″ beyond the stitching lines for seam allowances. Mark the stitching lines, the small dots (●), and squares (■). Placing the marked grainline on the fold of the fabric, cut two pieces for the bag and two for the lining.

Trace and transfer the embroidery design to the bag fabric, placing it in the position shown on the drawing. Using a single strand of white yarn, embroider with the stitches indicated. Where Satin Stitch sections adjoin, as in the main stem of the flower, work the individual segments in different directions so they will stand apart from their neighbors.

To maintain the curve of the carnation petals it is necessary to work a few Straight Stitches in among the Bokhara Couching threads at the outside edges. If carefully placed, they blend in and are not noticed. (See detail photo, page 115.)

Block the completed embroidery.

Stitch the handbag sections together, leaving an opening between the small dots (●) on each side. Turn. Press seam.

Stitch the lining pieces together, leaving the lower edge open between the small squares (■). Press seams open. Pin the top of the lining to the top of the bag, matching seams. Stitch. Trim seam allowance to ¼″. Turn through the opening in the lining. Close the opening in the lining with small invisible stitches. Turn the lining into the bag along the upper seam line and press the seam flat.

Stitch along the lines to form a casing for the drawstrings. If desired, trim the top edge with a row of widely spaced Back Stitches to hold the edge in place.

Cut cording in half and insert one drawstring through the casing, starting and finishing at one side opening. Draw the remaining cord through the casing in the same manner but starting and finishing in the other seam opening.

Overleaf: A closeup of part of the
pouch shows that embroidery on the
same-color background has enough
texture to make it stand on its own.
The stitches shown are Bokhara
Couching, French Knots, Satin
Stitch, and Trellis Couching. An additional photograph of the flower is
among the embroidery stitch illustrations at the back of the book.

113

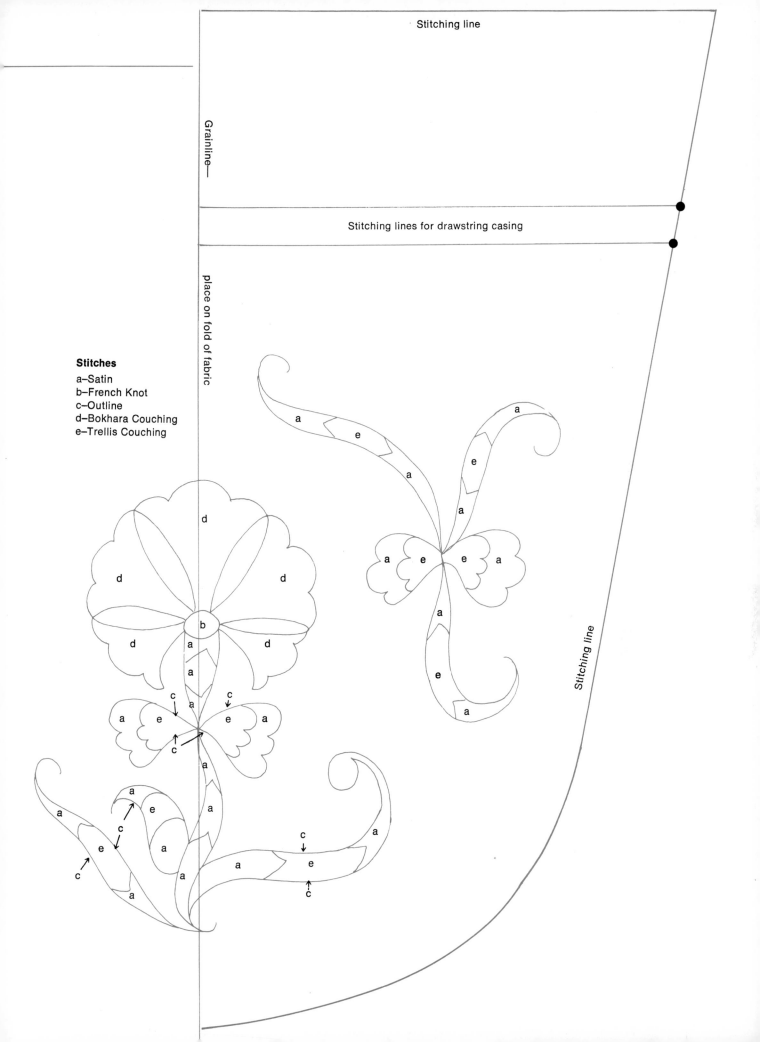

Stitching line

Grainline—

Stitching lines for drawstring casing

place on fold of fabric

Stitches

a–Satin
b–French Knot
c–Outline
d–Bokhara Couching
e–Trellis Couching

Stitching line

PETITE FLORAL SPRAYS

Little flowers in easy stitches and pretty colors make a trio of charming miniatures. A layer of Dacron quilt filler under the linen provides the slightly padded effect which is a nice alternative to the flat, stretched look so often seen in framed embroidery.

The little sprays would also be pretty if scattered on a sweater, and they can be used on placemats, tablecloths, or various other items of apparel.

Finished size: 4" × 5" oval
Materials: Three pieces of natural-colored linen each approximately 7" × 8"
Embroidery needle
DMC Embroidery Floss, 1 skein each: 727–soft yellow; 726–bright yellow; 444–yellow-gold; 741–orange; 471–light yellow-green; 472–pale yellow-green; 3346–dark avocado; white; 932–pale blue; 351–coral; 352–medium coral; 754–pale pink
Three oval frames 4" × 5"

Instructions: Trace the drawings and transfer them to the linen.

Buttercup: Work all stitches with three strands of floss. All flower petals are to be padded Satin Stitch, leaves Fishbone, and stems Outline Stitch. Work the centers in French Knots in a combination of orange and green for a shaded effect.

Daisy: Work the stitches with three strands of floss except for the Outline Stitch around the flower petals, which should be worked with a single strand. Make the stems Outline Stitch, leaves Fishbone, centers French Knots predominantly yellow with a few orange stitches for shading. The daisy petals are to be white padded Satin with an Outline Stitch edge of a single strand of pale blue.

Fuchsia: Embroider with three strands of floss except for outlines as noted. Finish flower petals and leaves in padded Satin in the colors noted on the chart. Work Outline Stitch around all petals with a single strand of 351 and around all leaves with a strand of 472. Work all stems in Outline Stitch. Stamens are to be Outline Stitch with a French Knot at the end.

Steam to block and frame as shown.

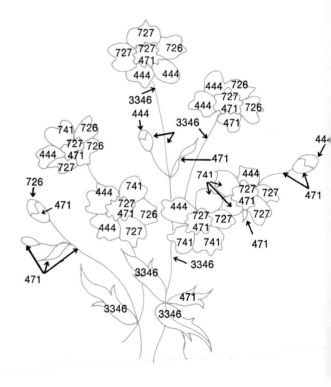

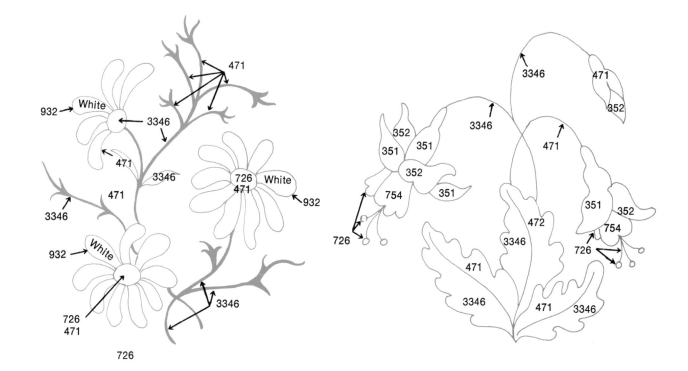

CREWEL BELL PULL

These five small multicolored early American design adaptations line up vertically on a linen bell pull. The typically colonial combination of shades of blue, gold, rose, rust, and green is colorful and bright but will coordinate with many color schemes. This one is backed with blue corduroy and finished with brass hardware and a large decorative tassel. A layer of Dacron quilt filler between the linen and corduroy gives the hanging a softer look than is usually used.

The individual flower motifs can be made into a set of small pictures with oval frames. There are also many other ways that small designs like this can be used.

The panel can be lengthened or shortened by changing the number of flowers. If greater length is needed, insert a mirror image of one or two motifs and rearrange both the sequence of the flowers and the color plan. Do not add more colors—just use the present ones differently.

Finished size: 6″ × 35″ (exclusive of hardware and tassel)
Materials: Natural-colored linen approximately 10″ × 39″
Crewel needle
Persian yarn, 5 yards each: 510–Medium Green; 555–Green Giant; 570–Celery Leaf; 334–Dark French Blue; 330–Old Blue; 385–French Blue; 395–Light Blue; 427–Medium Gold; 447–Mustard; 457–Canary Yellow; 467–Light Medium Yellow; 215–Cinnamon; 423–Pale Rust; 425*–Indian Pink; 234–Toasty Pink; 281–Antique Pink; 865–Powder Pink (* available in Paternayan only)
For tassel (if desired): 330–Old Blue, 1 extra skein

Appropriate lining fabric about 10″ × 39″
Dacron quilt filler approximately 6″ × 35″
Bell Pull hardware
Note 1: All embroidery is to be worked with a single ply of yarn.
Note 2: See detail photographs of individual motifs for help with the embroidery.

Instructions: Cut the linen carefully to make sure it is absolutely straight. Hem or zigzag the edges to prevent fraying. Trace the motifs and transfer to the linen, taking care to center them on the fabric. Place them as shown, always leaving a 2″ space between the lower edge of one and the top limit of the next.

(Full-size photograph appears on page 123)

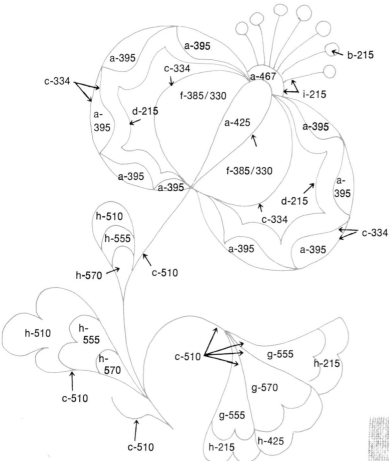

c-334
a-395
a-395
c-334
a-467
b-215
f-385/330
i-215
a-395
a-395
d-215
a-425
a-395
a-395
a-395
d-215
a-395
c-334
c-334
a-395
a-395

h-510
h-555
h-570
c-510

h-510
h-555
h-570
c-510
c-510
g-555
h-215
g-570
g-555
h-215
h-425
c-510

a—Satin
b—French
   Knots
c—Outline
d—Chain
e—Fishbone
f—Trellis
   Couching
g—Split
h—Buttonhole
i—Back
j—Long-and-Short
k—Lazy Daisy

Motif #1: Use the colors and stitches as noted on the chart. Make a cluster of five or six tiny French Knots to fill each of the small circles at the top of the flower.

The semicircles at the sides of the flower center are to be outlined with 334, then filled with Trellis Couching. Where two numbers appear (*"385/330,"* for example), the first number (*385*) is the color of the laid threads, while the second (*330*) denotes the color of the tie-down stitches. These last are small Straight Stitches which lie vertically across the intersections of the lattice.

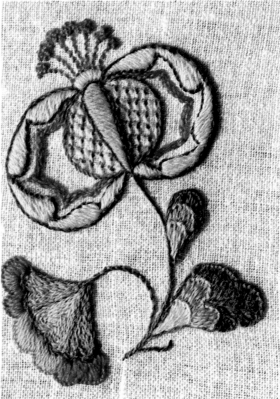

CREWEL BELL PULL

Motif #2: The two petals on either side of the top center of the flower are marked *"j-467, 457, 447, 427"* to indicate Long-and-Short shading from the palest gold at the outside to deep gold at the base of the petals.

The three petals that are marked *"f-457/330"* are Trellis Couching in 457 with the small vertical tiedown stitches in 330–Old Blue. The center petal is Long-and-Short shading from pale gold at the top to deepest at the base.

Work the Split Stitch leaves in very close rows, beginning at the outside edge and following the leaf shape until it is filled completely.

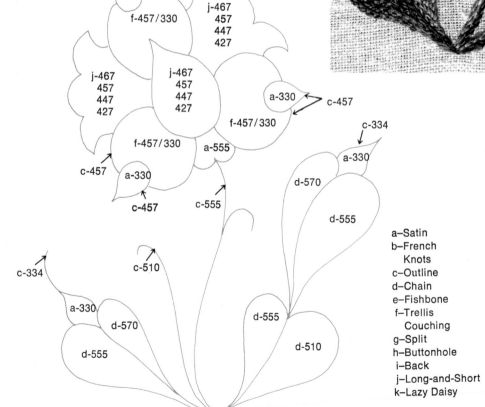

a–Satin
b–French
   Knots
c–Outline
d–Chain
e–Fishbone
f–Trellis
   Couching
g–Split
h–Buttonhole
i–Back
j–Long-and-Short
k–Lazy Daisy

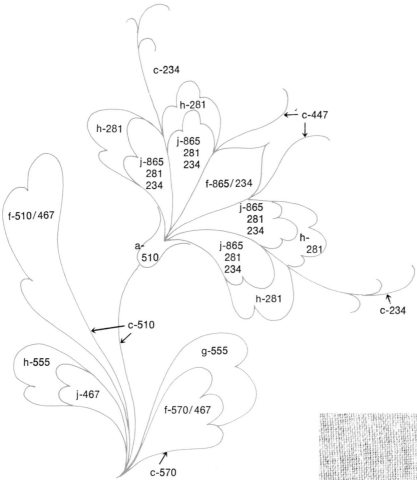

c-234

h-281

h-281

←— c-447

j-865
281
234

j-865
281
234

f-865/234

f-510/467

j-865
281
234

a-
510

j-865
281
234

h-
281

h-281

c-234

c-510

g-555

h-555

j-467

f-570/467

c-570

a—Satin
b—French
   Knots
c—Outline
d—Chain
e—Fishbone
f—Trellis
   Couching
g—Split
h—Buttonhole
i—Back
j—Long-and-Short
k—Lazy Daisy

Motif #3: The four flower petals
have a wide Buttonhole edge of color
281—Antique Pink. The remaining portions of the petals are Long-and-Short,
working from the palest pink to the deepest shade at the base. The center petal is
Trellis Couching, with the laid threads
and outline in 865—Powder Pink and the
tiedown stitches in 234—Toasty Pink.

   The long slender leaf at the right is
outlined in 510—Medium Green, and has
laid threads of the same green fastened
with small straight stitches of 467—Light
Medium Yellow. The small leaf directly
below has a border of Buttonhole and a
small section worked in Long-and-Short
in yellow. The upper section of the leaf at

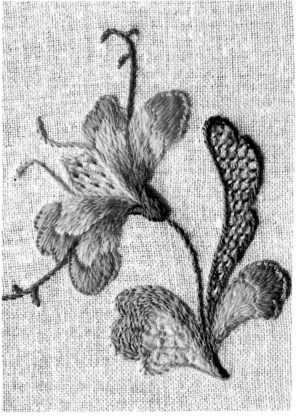

the left is worked in closely spaced rows of Split Stitch in 555–Green Giant. The lower portion of the leaf is Trellis Couching with the outline and laid threads in 570–Celery Leaf, while the tiedown threads are 467–Light Medium Yellow. In each diamond-shaped space of the Trellis Couching there is a yellow French Knot.

Motif #4: The two large winglike petals should first be outlined with Back Stitch in blue. The French Knots should then be worked in rows following the shape of the petals and beginning at the outside edges with the deepest shade of gold. Allow the first row of French Knots to overlap the blue outline slightly. Fill in

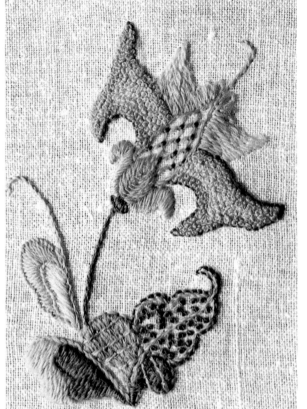

a–Satin
b–French
  Knots
c–Outline
d–Chain
e–Fishbone
f–Trellis
  Couching
g–Split
h–Buttonhole
i–Back
j–Long-and-Short
k–Lazy Daisy

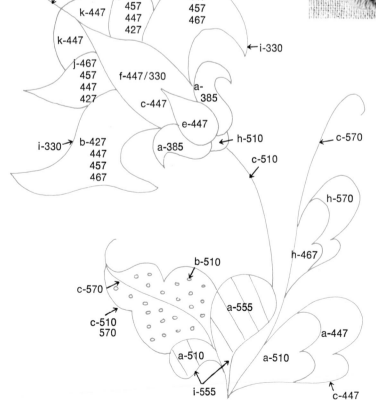

the entire petal with French Knots, working from the deepest shade of gold at the outside edge to the palest at the center.

The two small petals on either side of the center at the top are Long-and-Short, shading from the palest gold at the outside to the deepest at the base. In the semicircular sections immediately above these petals work six Lazy Daisy stitches in 447–Mustard. Fill the center of each of the loops with a Straight Stitch of 385–French Blue.

The center petal is Trellis Couching with laid threads and outline in 447–Mustard. The small tiedown stitches are 330–Old Blue.

The two lower sections of the leaf at the right are worked in Satin Stitch in 510 and 555, as noted on the chart. The two are then outlined with Back Stitch in 555, and a thread of 555 is laid across the Satin Stitch and fastened with small stitches of the same color. The remaining portion of the leaf is outlined with two rows of green and filled with a scattering of French Knots.

Motif #5: The three sections of this flower that are to be worked in Trellis Couching are outlined in Chain Stitch in 330–Old Blue. The laid threads are 385, with vertical tiedown stitches of 425–Indian Pink.

The leaves are worked in rows of Chain Stitch beginning with 510 at the outside edges and shading through the greens to yellow at the inside. There will be some linen visible at the centers. The larger of the leaves has Lazy Daisy loops on either side of the vein to partially fill the open space.

(Motif #5 is on the following page.)

CREWEL BELL PULL

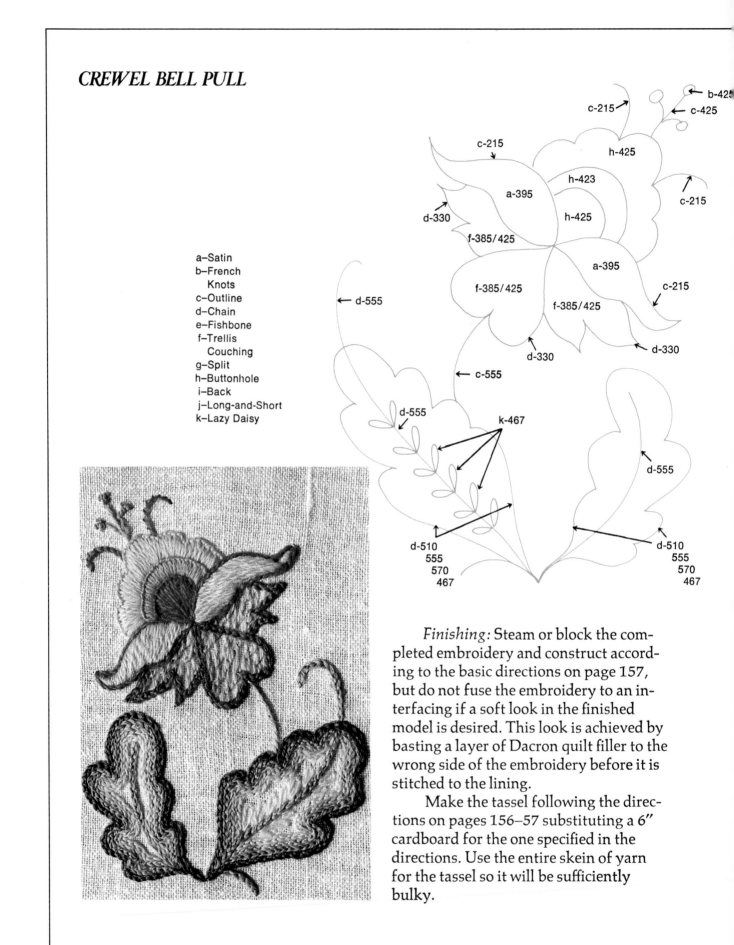

a–Satin
b–French
   Knots
c–Outline
d–Chain
e–Fishbone
f–Trellis
   Couching
g–Split
h–Buttonhole
i–Back
j–Long-and-Short
k–Lazy Daisy

Finishing: Steam or block the completed embroidery and construct according to the basic directions on page 157, but do not fuse the embroidery to an interfacing if a soft look in the finished model is desired. This look is achieved by basting a layer of Dacron quilt filler to the wrong side of the embroidery before it is stitched to the lining.

Make the tassel following the directions on pages 156–57 substituting a 6″ cardboard for the one specified in the directions. Use the entire skein of yarn for the tassel so it will be sufficiently bulky.

THE STITCHES

THE SURFACE STITCHES

Embroidery stitches are many and fascinating. Volumes have been devoted to the study of their origins, application, and classification. Old samplers recording numerous varieties of stitches fill drawers of textile museums as testament to the universal and unending interest in stitches and their variations. The modern embroidress has at her disposal a seemingly endless choice of stitches with which to experiment or enrich her work.

This rich resource of stitches can become a confusing tangle of meaningless techniques unless a discriminating choice is made. The sampler is still a very valuable tool: if stitches are learned and recorded on a reference piece, it is easy later to go back and choose the correct stitch for a particular area. Many of the best of the old needleworks are worked entirely in just a few limited stitches, and the effect is beautiful. Some of the lovely eighteenth-century American pieces are worked in only two stitches—Roumanian Couching and Outline were the favorites. Many prized embroideries contain only four or five stitches, and it is rare to find one that made use of great numbers. These skilled craftspersons learned early that a few stitches and a few colors carefully combined are more likely to produce a lovely design than a wild array of either or both. We can take a lesson from history and choose our stitches with discrimination and use each to its own best advantage.

There are literally hundreds of stitches and even more variations of stitches. It's fun to learn them and to read about their history and the people who probably first used them. This can become an absorbing hobby. It seems that the larger one's working repertoire of stitches, the easier it is to decide which stitch will best enhance a particular design.

From the vast number of stitches only a few have been utilized for the projects in this book, and thus only that small number has been charted for reference. Basically these are some of the easiest and therefore the most commonly used. Most will be familiar to all, but all are beautiful and useful. Most of the stitches used are also shown in the closeup detail photos on pages 136–43 and 148–52. These will be as valuable as the diagrams in learning new stitches or in perfecting techniques already learned, for they show how the worked stitch actually looks on the fabric. Take advantage of all the photographs, for they illustrate embroidery lessons in a way words can never equal.

For the sake of convenience, the stitches have been divided into *Surface Stitches* and *Canvas Stitches*. Basically, the only difference is that the former are usually worked on the fabric in a free manner, without regard for the weave or thread count, while the canvas stitches depend greatly on the regularity of the foundation material. There is of course some overlapping, since some stitches are as important in one category as in the other—the Cross Stitch, for example. The increasing trend toward using free embroidery stitches to enhance needlepoint also contributes to the difficulty in positively classifying stitches for only one use. All are to be freely interchanged as suits the needs of the embroiderer.

THE SURFACE STITCHES

Back Stitch

An easy outline stitch, Back Stitch makes a neat line of stitches that bear a close resemblance to the top of a row of machine stitching. The stitch can be used as a finishing edge or outline or may be worked in closely spaced rows to fill a large area.

To begin a row of stitches, bring the needle to the surface at *A*, which is one stitch length from the beginning of the row. Go down at *B* and back to the surface again at *C*. Pull the yarn through to form a small stitch. Insert the needle again at *A* and continue stitching for the required distance, keeping the stitches as uniform as possible.

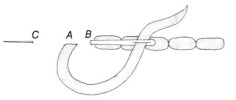

Bullion Stitch

Although it is a bit tricky at first, once mastered, the Bullion Stitch (or Bullion Knot) is a much-used stitch. It can be made to lie flat along a line, or to curve, or to form a rosebudlike cluster. Its coiled length makes an interesting raised flower center, or it can be used as a detail in many different situations.

To start bring the needle up at *A* and pull the yarn through. Go down at *B* and come back up again at *A*, but *do not pull the thread through.* Wrap the yarn around the needle until the length of the coil is roughly equal to the distance from *A* to *B*.

Hold the wrap firmly and pull the needle through the coil of yarn. Hold the wrap and pull the yarn all the way through so the stitch lies flat on the fabric. Take the needle to the wrong side at *B*, as in Step 2.

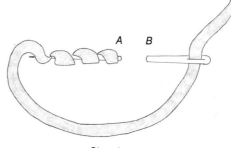

Step 1

Step 2

THE SURFACE STITCHES

Buttonhole Stitch

Sometimes called the Blanket Stitch, Buttonhole can be worked with the loops widely and evenly spaced, as shown on the diagram, or in many variations which group the stitches in decorative patterns. When the stitches are placed close together, they become an effective filling with a slightly raised self-edge.

To work, bring the needle up at *A* and pull the yarn through. Holding the yarn below the needle to form a loop, insert the needle into the fabric at *B* and bring it back to the surface at *C*. Pull the needle through, adjusting the tension of the loop to allow the stitch to lie flat. Continue in this manner.

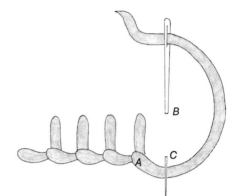

Chain Stitch

A single row of Chain Stitch forms a broad outline, while closely spaced rows following the form of a motif make an effective shaded filling.

To start, bring the needle up at *A*, pulling the thread through. Holding the yarn below the needle to form a loop, insert the needle again at *A* and bring the point up at *B*. Pull through and adjust the loop.

When working rows as a filling, begin by outlining the outside edge of the motif and progress toward the center, keeping all rows in the same direction and allowing the rows to flow in the same lines as the shape being filled. In the center, fill in any small section that will not accommodate full rows with portions of rows that fit.

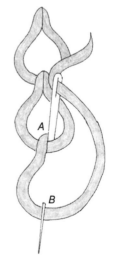

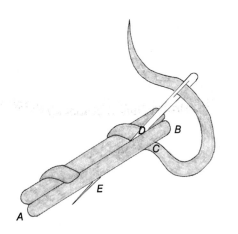

Couching

Couching, actually a method of fastening down long threads on the surface of the embroidery, appears in many variations and fills many purposes. It can make a delicate outline or any one of a dozen decorative fillings.

Hold the thread to be fastened—the *laid thread*—in position along the line to be outlined. Bring the needle threaded with another strand to the surface at *A* and insert it again at *B* on the other side of the laid thread. Pull through, forming the small stitch to hold the thread in place. These little Couching Stitches may be upright or slightly slanted as desired.

Rows of this form of Couching can also be used as a solid filling. When this is done, place the small stitches carefully, as they form a secondary pattern that can add greatly to the appearance of the embroidery.

Bokhara Couching

Bokhara Couching is a decorative filling stitch that is worked with a single strand of yarn making both the laid stitch and the tiedown. The threads are tied in a pattern which can be repeated as often as necessary. The flower petals on the white-on-white drawstring pouch on pages 112–15 have been worked in this method, since it fills the shape so well and avoids long threads that would snag. As noted in the instructions for the piece, it was necessary to add short stitches at the outside edge of the petals to make a curved shape, but these have been placed carefully and blend into the couching so well that they are not noticed.

(*Cont.*)

THE SURFACE STITCHES

Bokhara Couching (*cont.*)

To begin, lay the long stitch across the shape by bringing the needle to the surface at *A*, going down at *B*, and bringing the needle to the surface again at *C* as close as possible to the laid stitch. Take the needle down again at *D*, making the small slanted stitch across the long thread. (Two of these small slants are already shown finished.) Bring the needle to the surface at *E* and proceed to make the second couching stitch. Bring the needle back to the surface in position for the beginning of another long laid stitch and continue.

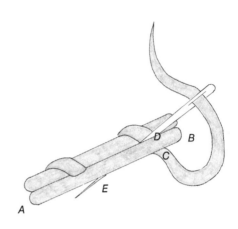

Trellis Couching

Trellis Couching quickly covers a large area with interesting pattern. The laid and couching threads can be of matching color or may be contrasting. The latter can take the simple form shown on the chart, or can be Cross Stitch, Lazy Daisy, or any one of a number of small stitches that would fasten the long threads. The square openings can be left plain, as shown, or decorated with a small detached stitch.

To begin, lay the long straight stitches in parallel lines, filling the shape of the motif. Bring the needle to the surface and make the small tiedown stitch at each intersection of the laid threads.

When Trellis Couching is used in this book, dual numbers separated by a slash (/) on the chart indicate that the thread to be laid is of the first color while the tiedown stitches are of the second color.

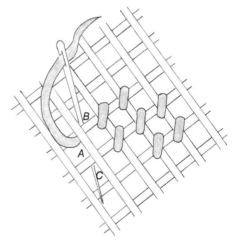

130

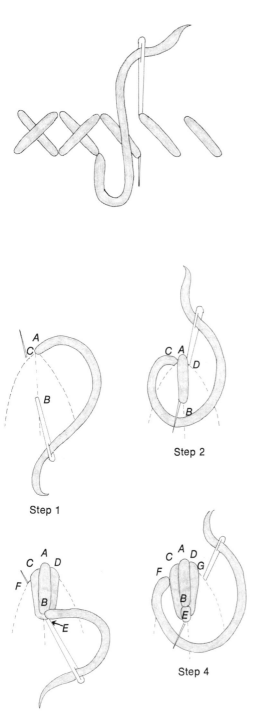

Step 1

Step 2

Step 3

Step 4

Cross Stitch

Equally at home on canvas or fabric, the Cross Stitch is very easy but nonetheless beautiful and effective.

The secret of lovely Cross Stitch is always to have the base stitches slanting in one direction throughout the work. When making multiple stitches in one color, it is best first to work across making the base stitches and then return, placing the second stitches on top as shown in the diagram. Single stitches can be completed individually.

Fishbone Stitch

The Fishbone Stitch is ideal filling for many floral forms and is thus a very-much-used crewel stitch. It can be worked solid (as in the diagram) or with the stitches widely spaced for an open effect.

The first stitch should be fairly long to insure that the side stitches lie on a good slant. To begin (Step 1), bring the needle up at A, pull the yarn through, and go down at B, which is about ¼" down the center line from A. Come up at C, which is to the left and very slightly below A on the outline. Holding the thread below the needle to form a loop (Step 2), go down at D, which corresponds to C but is to the right of A. Come up at B and pull the yarn through, adjusting the loop so the stitch lies flat. Make a small stitch across the loop by inserting the needle at E (Step 3). Come up at F on the left side and repeat the loop forming and the tie-down stitch (Step 4). Continue until area is covered.

A row of Split Stitch outlining the shape to be filled with Fishbone will impart a slightly raised appearance to the area and make it easy to maintain a smooth outside edge.

THE SURFACE STITCHES

French Knot

This interesting little knot serves many purposes; indeed, it would be hard to imagine embroidery without the charm of French Knots. They can be used separately as seeding, packed together to form solid textured areas, worked in rows of shaded colors, or grouped to make interesting flower centers or any number of other floral details.

To make the knot, bring the needle to the surface at *A* and pull the yarn through. Wrap the yarn around the needle once, then insert the tip of the needle into the fabric close to *A*, but with at least one thread of the fabric intervening. Pull the yarn to make the wrap fit snugly around the needle. Pull the needle through.

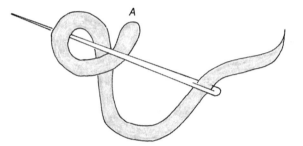

Lazy Daisy

The Lazy Daisy is often called the Detached Chain, which is a very accurate description of it. An easy stitch which can be used in a variety of ways, Lazy Daisy is probably familiar to all.

To work, bring the needle up at *A* and pull the yarn through. Holding the yarn below the needle to form a loop, go down again at *A* and bring the needle up to the surface at *B*. Pull the yarn through and adjust the loop. Make a small stitch across the loop at *B* to fasten.

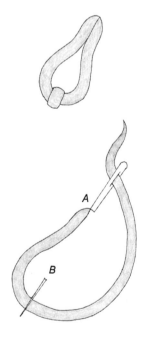

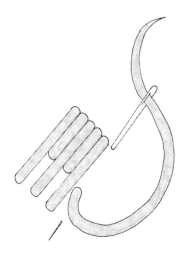

Long-and-Short Stitch

Any list of the basic crewel stitches would certainly have Long-and-Short among them, for this stitch produces shading and detail unequaled by any other. It may be worked in even rows or in an irregular pattern which produces a painted effect. The basic stitching foundation is the same for the two methods.

Only the first or outside row has both long and short stitches, a quirk that is often confusing to the beginner. To practice the stitch, use a heavy yarn and work the rows in contrasting colors so the stitches will be very clearly visible. Begin with a straightedge and make the long stitches ½″ and the short ones ¼″. Work a short row, placing the stitches close together as shown in the diagram. Change colors and work a row of long stitches in the slotted spaces by bringing the needle to the surface through the yarn at the base of each short stitch. For the next row change colors and work the row of long stitches in the slotted spaces produced by the previous row.

To work a curved line, begin the outside row at the middle of the curve and work the Long-and-Short Stitches to one side, then go back to the center and work to the other side. Stitches should overlap slightly and gradually change direction to fit an irregular shape.

An outline of Split Stitch around a motif to be worked in Long-and-Short will impart a raised appearance and a very smooth edge.

When Long-and-Short is used in this book all the colors used in the shaded area are listed in order in the motif on the chart. Thus a flower petal marked to be

THE SURFACE STITCHES

in Long-and-Short in colors 855 (Peony), 860 (Magnolia), and 865 (Powder Pink) would be worked shading the colors from dark to light using the three shades indicated. Use the detail photographs provided as a guide to shading and handle the colors much as paint to achieve a delicate transition from one value to the next.

Outline Stitch

Worked as shown in the diagram, with the yarn always above the needle, the Outline Stitch creates a fine line of very close stitches. When the yarn is held below the needle, the line is perceptibly broader and the stitches are slightly separated. Some embroiderers call the fine line the Stem Stitch and the latter the Crewel Stitch, but actually they are both the Outline.

 To begin a line of stitching, bring the needle to the surface at A and pull the yarn through. With the yarn above the needle, go down at B and come up at C, exactly halfway between A and B. Pull the yarn through and continue stitching.

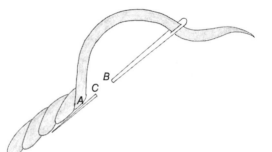

Satin Stitch

One of the loveliest of the embroidery stitches, Satin is aptly named, for when properly worked it has a smooth, lustrous look. A Split Stitch outline adds depth and eases the task of making an even outside edge. Extra padding in the form of long stitches can be added if desired.

 To work as diagrammed, outline the area with small Split Stitch in the same yarn that will be used for the Satin Stitch. Bring the needle up at A. Go down at B

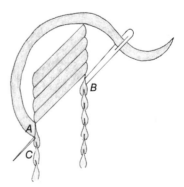

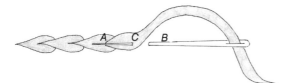

on the opposite side and far enough above *A* to create a good slant. Come back up at *C*, just below *A*, pull yarn through and continue stitching, adjusting length of stitches to fit shape of area being filled.

Split Stitch

Hardworking little Split Stitch, which looks like a scaled-down version of the Chain Stitch, does many embroidery jobs. It is a lovely fine outlining stitch, is often used as a padding for other stitches, and can be worked in closely spaced rows as a filling for large areas.

To work, bring the needle to the surface at *A* and go down at *B*. Pull the yarn through to form a small, flat stitch. Bring the needle up at *C*, halfway between *A* and *B*, piercing the stitch.

Straight Stitch

The Straight Stitch is an uncomplicated flat stitch often used as an accent or scattered as seeding to add texture to a large otherwise plain area. The slant and size of the stitches can vary to suit the need at hand. To work, simply place the stitches at the desired angle following the stitching order from *A* to *B* to *C*.

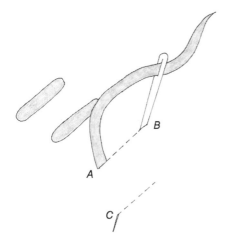

135

THE SURFACE STITCHES

Closely placed rows of Chain Stitch working from dark green to progressively lighter values effectively shade a shapely oak leaf. The rows follow the outline of the leaf to emphasize its graceful curves. The center portion is, in the colonial manner, left unworked. Other stitches used on the detail are Long-and-Short for petals and Lazy Daisy and Split Stitch at the base of the flower. (Detail from Carnation and Oak Leaf Picture.)

Long-and-Short Stitches "paint" flower petals to best advantage—palest shade at the outside edge, deepest at the center. The three petals in Trellis Couching with Satin Stitch at the tips combine with the shaded petals to create a flower Mother Nature would never recognize. Outline Stitch in color matching the Trellis Couching makes a smooth uniting edge. (Detail of one motif of the Crewel Bell Pull.)

Rows of tiny Split Stitch fit neatly into the curving outlines of a leaf to produce a delicate shading. Chain Stitch outlines another portion of the leaf the center of which is filled with scattered French Knots. (Detail of the Green Linen Pillow.)

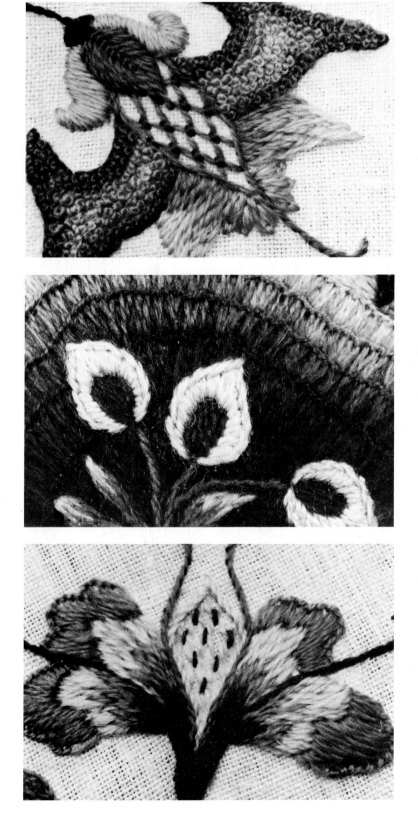

Tiny French Knots in closely spaced rows completely fill the petals of a Jacobean flower. The first row of knots was worked to partially overlap a row of blue Back Stitch which forms a narrow, shadowlike outline. Trellis Couching fills the flower center, while the base is formed by a petal of gold Fishbone with a curving blue Satin Stitch leaf shape at each side. Petals at the top are Long-and-Short with a crown of six Lazy Daisy Stitches which have a single blue Straight Stitch as filling. (Detail from a motif on the Crewel Bell Pull.)

Buttonhole Stitch can cover a large area and maintain a flowing line very effectively, as seen here. The flowers are worked in two shades of rose and are finished with a row of Outline Stitch. The leaves are Long-and-Short, stems Outline Stitch worked over the Buttonhole Stitch background.

This pretty rose-colored flower combines Buttonhole, Long-and-Short, Trellis Couching, Satin Stitch, and Outline. Each stitch performs at its best in the graceful shape. (Detail from the Crewel Bell Pull.)

THE SURFACE STITCHES

A modern version of an early American Jacobean-style flower has Satin Stitch forming the center and the blue curves at the outside. Trellis Couching is a light filling for the large semicircular areas on either side of the center. Outline Stitch makes a neat edge which unites the sections into one flower. Open spaces and fanciful shape are typical of eighteenth-century flowers.

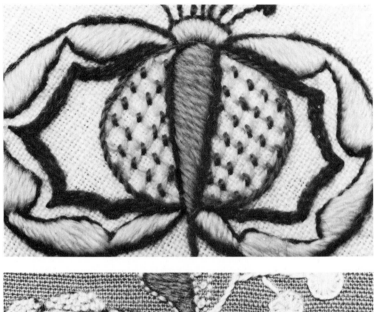

An interesting flower worked in beiges on green uses rows of Buttonhole in three pale shades as a filling for the wide base. Groups of Straight Stitches fill the open area which is rimmed with curved shapes in Satin Stitch which had been outlined with Back Stitch. The outside is edged with Outline Stitch in a deep brown, and the scalloped petals are filled with tiny French Knots.

    The leaf shown has been worked in Satin, Outline, and Back Stitches with a scattering of French Knots as filling for one section. (Detail from Green Linen Pillow.)

This closeup of a flower reveals a central leaf worked in brown Trellis Couching with tiedown Cross Stitches of blue and French Knots of the same blue at the center of each diamond. Directly below is a row of irregular gold Buttonhole outlining a petal, while the space at the upper left is filled with tiny Straight Stitch seeding. A wider outline of slanted gold Satin Stitch finishes the flower shape. The brown and yellow leaf at right is Split Stitch worked in closely spaced rows.

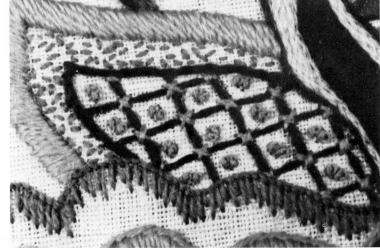

Tiny pastel flowers worked in cotton embroidery floss take advantage of many decorative stitches. Satin Stitch, Buttonhole Stitch, and Bullion Knots form the flowers, while French and Bullion Knots fill the centers. The leaves are Fishbone Stitch in two shades of green.

Little flowers grouped informally as in a summer garden are worked in the pastels of the season in Satin, Buttonhole, and Long-and-Short Stitch with French Knot centers. The barely visible leaves are Fishbone.

These plump strawberries are worked in Satin Stitch with Trellis Couching worked on top. The leaves are Fishbone. (Detail from the Green Linen Pillow.)

THE SURFACE STITCHES

This Satin Stitch bumblebee has a striped body, antennae of Bullion Stitch, finishing details of Straight Stitch, and an Outline Stitch edge. (Detail from the Green Linen Pillow.)

Detail enlargement of the Pennsylvania Dutch Birth Certificate shows clearly the luster and beauty of stitches worked in cotton embroidery floss. The Diestelfink's body is Chain Stitch; the head and tail are Satin Stitch, while Trellis Couching fills the wing. Flowers are worked in Satin and Outline Stitches with French Knot centers and Fishbone leaves.

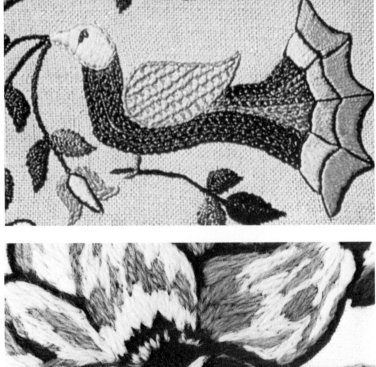

Flower worked on a printed fabric in Long-and-Short Stitch with a Split Stitch outline has a cluster of French Knots for a center. The color of the yarn used for stitching was matched as closely as possible to the fabric print, and the shading on the original flower was used as a guide for color placement in the embroidery. (Detail from the Bird Pillow.)

140

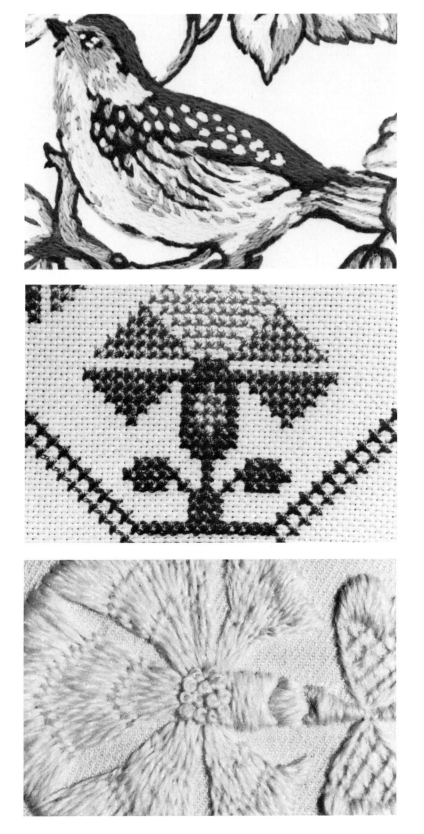

Bird worked on a printed drapery fabric in colors matching the fabric is lightly textured with Long-and-Short Stitch worked in a random manner. (Detail from the Bird Pillow.)

The traditional carnation or pink is a favorite often appearing among the old motifs on Cross Stitch samplers. This version from the Gardener Sampler is worked in three shades of pink on Hardanger fabric, which provides an excellent foundation for counted Cross Stitch.

Detail from the White-on-White Drawstring Pouch shows that a pattern can be effectively detailed with only one color. Stitches worked in wool over a Split Stitch outline have the dimension and texture to make them stand apart from a background of the same color. Bokhara Couching on the petals has been shaped to the flower outline by placing the tiedown strategically in double rows, which add a bonus effect. The other stitches shown are French Knots, Trellis Couching, Satin, and Outline.

THE SURFACE STITCHES

This detail from the Pennsylvania Dutch Birth Sampler shows the glowing colors of cotton embroidery floss in stitches often reserved for crewelwork. The stitches are much smaller than when worked with yarn, but just as lovely and effective.

This view of a leaf shows the use of Split Stitch in closely spaced rows to fill space completely. Shading is accomplished by using two lighter greens in the top section, darker shades at the bottom. The navy vein is Outline Stitch, while the small gold tip is worked in Satin Stitch with the navy Outline Stitch continuing around it. This makes a graceful leaf. (Detail is from Crewel Bell Pull.)

Blue leaves "painted" with Long-and-Short Stitch are outlined with Split Stitch in the deepest shade of blue. The vine is also worked in Split Stitch in tightly spaced rows to make a textured but flowing line.

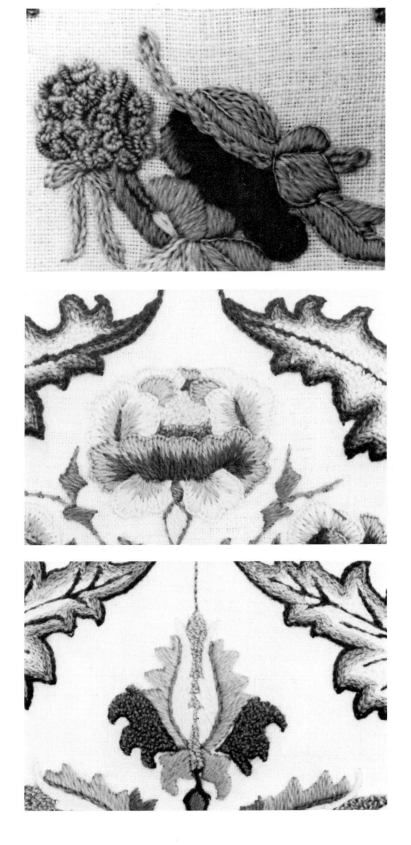

A little girl dressed in her Sunday best is worked predominantly in Satin Stitch with details of Outline and Couching of embroidery floss. The bouquet of flowers is made of Bullion and French knots.

The Buttonhole Stitch combines with Long-and-Short to shade and differentiate the petals of a rose. The center is solid French Knots in three shades of yellow gold, while the leaves are worked in Chain Stitch and more French Knots.

This interesting gold flower is worked in Satin Stitch and French Knots. Split Stitch padding under the Satin Stitch adds depth which details of Outline and Back Stitches accentuate. The leaves are closely spaced rows of Split Stitch.

THE CANVAS STITCHES

Tent Stitch

Whenever needlepoint is mentioned, Tent Stitch, which is the basic canvas stitch, comes immediately to mind. The stitch is oval in shape and always slants upward from lower left to upper right and fits so closely to its neighbors that it completely covers the canvas and creates the prized fabric which is needlepoint. This versatile and practical stitch can be used alone or in combination with other stitches to accent their showy textures.

Three methods of working the Tent Stitch—the Basket Weave, the Continental, and the Half Cross—have been used in making the projects in this book. All are probably already familiar to the reader but have been diagrammed for reference. Although it is always best to use the stitch recommended for each project, the Basket Weave and Continental may be freely interchanged, as the yarn requirements are the same for both stitching methods. However, if either of the latter is substituted for the Half Cross, it is necessary to add a quarter more yarn to the quantity listed in the materials for any project.

The *Basket Weave Stitch* does not cause as much stretching of the canvas as the Continental, and is therefore much favored by those who have mastered its technique. It is a bit tricky to work in the beginning, but not nearly as difficult as it is believed to be. Try it first within the confines of a square shape until you understand the stitching pattern, then try working an irregular shape. Often it is a help to outline the irregular shape with Continental and then work the Basket Weave within the outline.

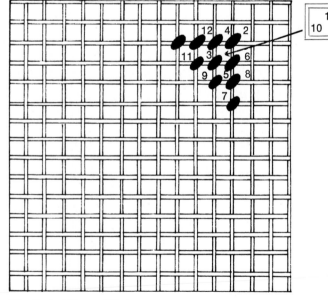

The Basket Weave Stitch

144

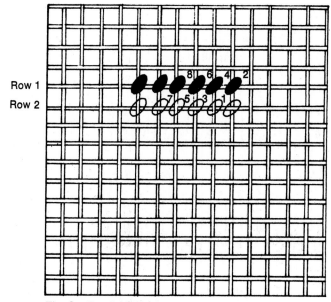

Row 1
Row 2

The Continental Stitch

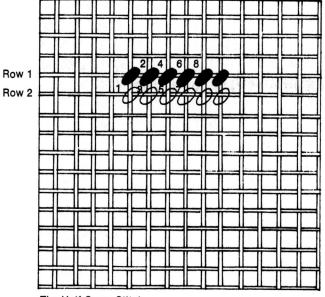

Row 1
Row 2

The Half Cross Stitch

Practice on a small piece of canvas beginning at the upper right corner with the first stitch and work following the numbers in the diagram. Note that after a few rows have been worked, there is a definite woven pattern on the back. The rows will be diagonal and will alternate— one row worked upward followed by one row in the downward direction, and so on. Keep up this sequence to maintain an even texture in the stitches.

The *Continental Stitch* is worked in rows across the canvas beginning at the top right side. The row is worked in the numbered sequence shown in the diagram. When the end of the row is reached, the canvas is turned and the return row worked as shown by the outlined stitches in Row 2.

Both of these Tent Stitches are well padded on the back, making them practical for most needlepoint projects. They use the same quantities of yarn and can be substituted for one another in instructions that call for either.

The *Half Cross Stitch* is worked from left to right across the canvas in rows in a stitching pattern that places only a minimum of yarn on the back of the work. This is often advantageous as the fabric is not as heavy and bulky as that produced by the Basket Weave and Continental Stitches; there is also a saving of yarn.

Begin the row at the upper left, bringing the needle to the surface at 1 and stitching following the numbered sequence on the chart to the end of the row. Turn the canvas so the bottom of the piece is at the top and work the return row as shown by the outlined stitches of Row 2, exercising care not to split the stitches of Row 1 as the needle comes to the surface.

THE CANVAS STITCHES

Upright Gobelin Stitch

Bargello is based on the Upright Gobelin Stitch, using variations in how it is placed on the canvas. When worked across the canvas in rows, as diagrammed, the Upright Gobelin creates a strong horizontal line. The stitch length can vary according to need; stitches sewn over 2 to 6 threads are the most practical. This stitch is widely used in this book as a device for creating border patterns, but it can also be used as background or for other decorative needs.

When the Upright Gobelin is used as a border, it is especially attractive worked over a traumé thread, which adds a raised or padded effect. To work the stitch thus, make the stitch as in the chart, but work over a three-ply strand of yarn in matching color held in place under the stitches. The Upright Gobelin will keep the thread in place, eliminating the necessity to stitch the traumé through the canvas. This is the best method, as most fastening stitches create irregularities in the weight of the padding.

Emphasize the raised appearance and cover any canvas threads visible between rows of Upright Gobelin with a row of Back Stitch worked with a single strand of matching yarn between the rows.

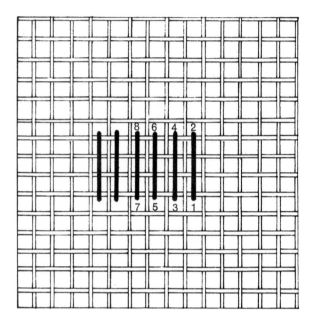

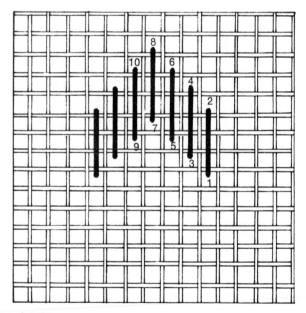

4-1 Step

146

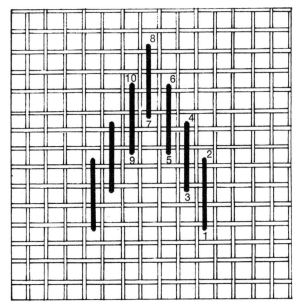

4-2 Step

Bargello Stitch

Bargello designs are created when Upright Gobelin Stitches are placed so they move up or down the canvas in rows. When the stitches are 4 threads long and each is placed 1 thread above or below the last, the arrangement is called a *4-1 step*. As the diagram shows, this forms a line of compact stitches with a gentle diagonal slope.

Similarly, when the stitches are 4 threads long and placed 2 threads above or below the last, the line is referred to as a *4-2 step*. This placement results in a narrower line with a steeper slant.

Brick Stitch

The Brick Stitch is the Upright Gobelin again, this time arranged so that the stitches are alternately 2 threads up and 2 down, creating a brick pattern. Because it is another upright stitch, it fits well into many Bargello designs; but it is also an easy quick background stitch for busy patterns.

As noted before, there are many more canvas and surface stitches than have been diagrammed here. Naturally, any other stitches can be used in the projects shown, but in these cases allowance for additional yarn should usually be made, since many use greater yardage.

THE CANVAS STITCHES

This detail of a larger crewelpoint piece shows a Diagonal Scotch Stitch background with a variety of surface stitches. Shown are Whipped Spider-web, Long-and-Short, Bullion and French Knots, Outline, and Buttonhole.

A closeup view of a yellow daisy shows how efficiently clustered French Knots cover canvas and create a raised flower center. The yellow petals are the Diagonal Mosaic Stitch with an outline of Couching in a darker shade of yellow.

This tiny Tent Stitch flower has an outline of Couching to round the edges of the petals and an interesting center made of three Bullion Knots.

A yellow daisy worked in Diagonal Mosaic Stitch is given rounded petals provided by an outline of Couching in a deeper shade of yarn. Center is a solid cluster of French Knots worked in orange and green. (This and other stitches that are not diagramed are not necessary to work the projects in this book.)

Long-and-Short Stitch in yarn colors ranging from yellow to deep orange make an interesting flower on canvas. A cluster of French Knots forms a textured center. If this type of embroidery is to be used, it is best to work the background canvas stitches first so the free stitches can extend slightly into them. This covers the canvas completely and gives a raised appearance to the embroidery.

Pansy "face" is given detail and texture by the addition of surface embroidery stitches on top of Tent Stitch. Simple Straight Stitches add lavender "whiskers," while Bullion and French Knots form a raised center. (Detail of Pansy Picture.)

THE CANVAS STITCHES

This detail of the Bargello pattern for the Gold Chair shows clearly the soft shading and the stitch placement. To keep the overall color of the chair light, the paler shades of gold have been repeated more often than the deeper tones.

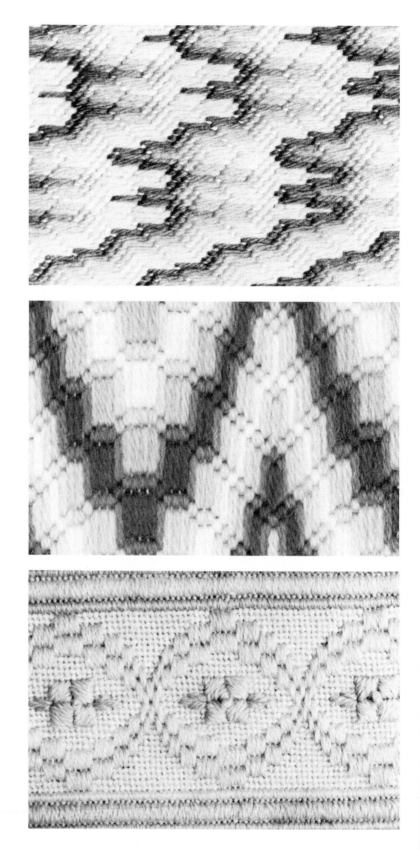

Bargello stitches in two lengths—long ones over 6 threads, short ones over 2 threads—and a monochromatic color scheme work up quickly to form a pleasing pattern. (Detail from the Florentine Swag Pillow.)

Bargello stitches are combined with Tent and Satin to make this pretty border. The small Satin Stitch flowers are worked over the Tent Stitch and are slightly raised. Straight Stitches form leaves, and a single yellow French Knot is the flower center. Back Stitch is shown between the rows of Upright Gobelin at the lower edge. (Detail of Nostalgic Pastel Pillow.)

Detail of a larger piece shows flowers worked in Diagonal Mosaic, Smyrna Cross, Tent, Mosaic, Encroaching Gobelin, Upright Cross, and Double Cross Stitch. All are outlined with Couching, which rounds the edges and covers awkward spots where stitches join. Centers are a variety of surface embroidery stitches, including Whipped Spiderweb, Turkey Work, and French Knots.

Bright shades of yellow, orange, green, and white translate a European folk embroidery motif into a charming contemporary Bargello repeat. The upright Bargello stitches adapt easily to many of the counted ethnic designs with results very much like this.

This small butterfly was worked entirely in Tent Stitch, then outlined with a single strand of black Couching to round the curves of the wings and add details.

151

THE CANVAS STITCHES

Butterfly on canvas is worked entirely
in Couching and Satin Stitch. Placing
the tiedown stitches strategically ac-
centuates the shape and line.

Another graceful butterfly on canvas
is embroidered in Couching, Fishbone,
Tent, and French Knots. Couching allows for rounded lines not possible
with Tent Stitch.

FINISHING

FINISHING

Almost as important as the quality of craftsmanship in a piece of embroidery is the degree of professionalism with which it is finished. The finishing process includes blocking, mounting, framing, or sewing construction, as required. Each technique exacts high standards of skill and attention to detail, but all are within the limits of reasonably talented persons willing to work with the care and precision that good needlework deserves.

Of course, all these services are available from professional craftsmen, but since they involve hand labor, they are necessarily expensive if well done. If the embroidery is of heirloom quality or is otherwise notable—perhaps a gift of special significance—professional finishing is probably indicated and certainly worth the price. For the myriad of lesser things most of us produce by the score, home finishing is usually more practical, economical, and satisfying. There is really an added sense of accomplishment inherent in being able to carry out a project from the beginning stitch to the final nail in the frame.

BLOCKING

Embroidery on Fabric
Even a piece of embroidery that has miraculously been completed while maintaining its new appearance needs a final steaming or blocking. Solid or wrinkled pieces need more attention, but even the most disreputable usually emerge from the blocking process looking new and fresh.

The equipment necessary for good blocking is not expensive and is often already on hand. The list includes a blocking board, rustproof tacks, T-square,

hammer, and either one of the new little steaming devices designed for home sewers or a steam iron that produces a good jet of steam. The little steamers are wonders, for they will not scorch fabric or flatten stitches but produce enough steam to even out stitches and dampen fabrics slightly.

New blocking devices designed especially for embroidery are very easy to use and simplify the process considerably. Many different models are on the market, ranging widely in price. If you plan to do a lot of blocking, you may want to investigate some of these products.

If the embroidery is clean, fasten it dry to the blocking board with the stitches facing up. Pull the fabric taut and fasten it firmly. Steam thoroughly and allow to dry on the board. (If the steamer is not available, dampen the fabric evenly with an atomizer or sponge.)

Soiled embroidery should be washed in cold water with mild soap. Agitate gently to remove soil, but try not to rub. Do not leave to soak. Rinse thoroughly—as many times as necessary until the water is clear—as soap residue can be very damaging over a period of years. Do not wring, but roll the piece in an absorbent towel and squeeze out excess moisture. Fasten the wet embroidery to the blocking board with the right side up. Pull the fabric taut and use the T-square to make certain it is straight. Allow the piece to dry. This is the best and most desirable method of blocking, especially when the embroidery is heavily worked or has large textured stitches.

Although as a general rule it is best to avoid using an iron to block embroidery, many flat pieces can be successfully blocked with one. If the piece is soiled, wash it as above. Roll up a clean piece in a damp towel until it is evenly moistened. Pad the ironing table with a double thickness of heavy terry toweling and iron the wrong side of the embroidery until it is dry, pulling the fabric as necessary to straighten it. The heavy padding will maintain the texture of the stitches. Never touch the iron to the right side of the embroidered piece.

Embroidery on Canvas

Most needlepoint is out of shape and needs wet blocking to restore its new look and to smooth the stitches. To wet the canvas and yarn evenly, roll it up in a towel that has been wet in cold water and let it stand overnight. Fasten the dampened canvas to the blocking board, pulling as necessary to straighten, checking with the T-square and placing the rustproof tacks about 1" apart. Leave the canvas on the blocking board to dry thoroughly. Drying times will vary, but the piece should not be removed until it is completely dry or it will revert to its unblocked shape.

Pieces that are worked entirely in the Tent Stitch can be blocked with the right side to the board or with the right side facing up according to individual preference in the appearance of the stitches. When placed with the right side to the board, the stitches are slightly flattened and very smooth. Stitches that are face up are still smooth, but have a more rounded appearance. Crewelpoint pieces should always be blocked right side facing up to preserve the depth and texture of the crewel stitches. Bargello is prettier when the stitches are more rounded, as they are when placed on the blocking board facing up.

Since Bargello stitches do not pull the canvas out of shape, many completed pieces need only be fastened to the blocking board and steamed. Again, the little triangular steamer is ideal, as it produces plenty of steam to loft the wool but will not scorch or flatten the stitches. The piece also dries very quickly after this treatment and will maintain its shape as well as a piece blocked by the conventional wet blocking method. If you substitute a steam iron for the steamer, do not allow the iron to rest on the Bargello at any time.

Bargello that is badly misshapen and crumpled should be blocked by the wet method described above. This method is also often best for pieces combining both Bargello and Tent Stitch sections, since the Tent Stitch has a tendency to distort the canvas.

Crewelpoint should be blocked wet, just as needlepoint, since it is generally out of shape. As noted above, place crewelpoint on the blocking board with the right side up to avoid flattening the crewel stitches.

Occasionally it seems impossible to straighten a piece of needlepoint on the blocking board. This usually happens with those pieces worked in the Continental Stitch. Pull and tack until it is as straight as possible. Allow it to dry and repeat the entire blocking procedure again. It will usually work out the second time and will be much easier than it was the first time. Good blocking is essential to good construction, for there is no way to sew a crooked piece of needlepoint into a square pillow, and no way to make a lopsided picture look right in a frame.

FINISHING

CONSTRUCTION

Pillows

Approach the task of making a pillow with the attitude that the embroidery—either on fabric or canvas—is an expensive piece of material which should be handled with reasonable care but is not so precious that one should be afraid to try to finish it. A pillow is a relatively easy sewing project requiring basic skills and care but no extraordinary ability. If you have never made one, it may be a good idea to purchase an extra half-yard of backing fabric and make a companion pillow before working with the embroidery. That way you'll gain confidence and expertise—and a complimentary pillow.

The materials needed for making a pillow are: appropriate fabric for the back; cable cord (a soft white cord from the drapery department); polyester fiber filling or a pillow form 1" larger than the finished pillow is to be in both dimensions; and matching thread. Use the zipper foot on the machine for professional-looking results.

Trim the unworked borders of the blocked needlepoint to ⅝". Using this as a pattern, cut the fabric backing to the same dimensions. Cut a length of cable cord 1" longer than the total distance around the sides of the trimmed embroidery for the pillow top. Cut a 1¼"-wide bias strip as long as the cable cord. Cut on the true bias, and piece the strip if necessary. Fold the bias strip in half lengthwise, insert the cable cord into the fold, and stitch as close as possible to the cord to make self-piping for insertion into the seams of the pillow.

With the embroidered pillow top right side up and beginning at the center of the bottom edge, pin the finished piping along the edge of the last row of stitches (if needlepoint or Bargello) or ⅝" from the raw edge of fabric. Pin the cording with the cut edges along the raw edges of the fabric or canvas. Clip the cording at the corners so a sharp right angle turn can be made. Overlap the ends of piping and lead them toward the raw edges. Machine-stitch in place, stitching as close as possible to the cord.

Place the fabric for the back on a flat surface right side up. Position the embroidery on top with wrong side up. Pin the layers together. Sew together on the line of stitching holding the piping in place. Leave the bottom partially open to receive filling. Trim seams and corners. Turn right side out. Fill with loose fiber filling or purchased pillow form. Slip-stitch to close opening.

Pincushions

A sachet or pincushion is only a tiny pillow, and the basic construction method is the same. Proceed as in the above instructions and insert lace, tassels, or other trimmings in the seam as desired. To use as a sachet, fill with dried flowers instead of fiber filling.

YARN TASSELS

Tassels are a luxurious finishing touch for many needlepoint and embroidery projects. They can be made of one accent color, or a combination of colors. The length and thickness can vary to suit any project, but basic construction is the same for all sizes.

Cut a piece of cardboard as wide as the desired length of the tassel. Wind the yarn around the cardboard as many times as necessary to achieve the thickness wanted for the tassel. If more than one tassel is to be made, count the times the yarn encircles the cardboard so all can be uniform weight.

Cut a length of yarn approximately 12" long. Double it and slip it under the yarn on the cardboard. Tie firmly at the top and slip the yarn off the cardboard. Leave the ends of the tie to be used to attach the tassel to the pillow or other project.

Tightly wrap another length of yarn around the tassel about ½" below the tie. Knot and pull the ends to the inside to hide them. Trim bottom loops of tassel to a neat, straight edge.

To use as trimming on a pillow, pin the tassels in place at the corners of the embroidery after the self-piping has been stitched in place. Continue with pillow construction, catching the yarn ends of the ties in the seam.

FINISHING A BELL PULL OR WALL HANGING

Successful finishing of a bell pull, wall hanging, or panel depends heavily on precise blocking. This cannot be overemphasized, for no matter how skillful the construction, the finished piece will be a failure if the embroidery was not perfectly straight. Block carefully—twice if necessary. Use a T-square or triangle to check corners to make certain they are square, and allow the piece to remain on the blocking board until it is completely dry. Use just as much care in cutting the lining or backing on the straight of the fabric. Take precautions to avoid any-

thing that would cause the hanging to be crooked as it hangs on the wall.

The materials used will vary according to the design of the embroidery. Generally needed are fabric for backing and either bell pull hardware or a dowel arrangement for hanging support. Tassels and self-piping can be used as trim if desired. Appropriate fabrics include velveteen, corduroy, upholstery-weight linen, and the luxurious new synthetic suedes.

If the hanging is needlepoint worked on a soft canvas or embroidery on fabric, it should be fused to one of the iron-on interfacings to give it body. The weight of the interfacing should be based on the amount of stiffening needed. Keep the piece pliable enough to handle and firm enough to hang well without making it stiff and hard.

Trim the borders of the needlepoint or embroidery to ⅝". Using this as a pattern, cut the backing the same size. Cut the interfacing the size of the embroidery minus the ⅝" seam allowance. Fuse the interlining to the embroidery, following the instructions with the product selected and being careful not to flatten the embroidery stitches with too much pressure from the iron.

If a self-piping is to be used, make it following the instructions with pillow construction (see page 156) and pin it in place along the seam line. Clip the piping at the corners so a sharp turn can be made if needed. Sew the piping in place using the zipper foot on the machine.

Lay the fabric for the back on a flat surface right side up. Place the embroidery on top of the backing fabric with the wrong side up. Pin the two together.

FINISHING

Stitch, using the row of machine stitches holding the piping in place as a guide. To avoid wrinkling the embroidery when the piece is turned right side out, stitch only one long side and across the bottom of the piece. Trim the seam allowance and the corner and turn. Pull out the corner to a neat square and press the seam. Turn to the inside and press the remaining edges and hand-sew to close. Attach bell pull hardware or dowel arrangement as needed.

FINISHING THE EYEGLASSES CASE

For the lining of an eyeglasses case choose soft, lint-free fabric that will add a small amount of protection for the glasses as well as a touch of luxury. Velveteen and corduroy are both good choices.

Trim the unworked borders of the blocked embroidery to ½" on all sides. Using the trimmed piece as a pattern, cut the lining. With right sides together, fold the lining in half so it will correspond to the shape of the finished case. Sew the bottom and side seams. Trim seam allowances to ⅛", but do not turn the lining.

With the steam iron, carefully press all seam allowances of the needlepoint or embroidery to the wrong side. If the piece is needlepoint, turn back part of the stitches of the last row so no canvas will be visible when the case is assembled.

With matching yarn or thread, beginning at the bottom edge and working from the right side, whip the case together as far as the corner. Insert the lining and continue joining to the top of the case. Turn to inside the seam allowance at top of lining and whip to edge of case.

FRAMING

There is much discussion about proper framing of embroidery, and many an effort to establish inflexible rules about the use of glass and mats. Many of these discussions omit the fact that there is more than one correct way to frame a given piece, and they fail to suggest that each piece should be considered in the light of personal preference as well as artistic value before any decision is made about framing materials. Styles in embroidery vary so greatly that many finishing techniques are needed to be certain that the correct look is achieved for each piece. While one piece may need a colored mat and classic frame, another may benefit from a wide, ornate frame, and still another may be shown to greatest advantage in an elegant oval. One may look best stretched tightly against a flat surface, while another needs a soft, padded look. The list could go on and on, but the essence is that the choice should be carefully considered and should complement —not overpower—the embroidery.

One of the biggest questions involves the use of glass over embroidery. In most instances it is best to frame without glass. While glass protects the embroidery from airborne dirt, it also obscures texture and may flatten stitches. Etched glareproof glass slightly darkens colors. Most dust can be easily brushed from the surface of an embroidered picture without damage to the stitches, but in areas where there is extreme pollution there is just no alternative to the use of glass or protection. Even when glass is used, embroidery should be removed from the frame and washed every three to five years to prevent rot.

A mat often highlights a picture by accenting a color or simply by adding to the overall size. New mats covered in textures simulating linen, burlap, silk, and grass cloth are unusually attractive with needlework. Plain board mats covered with fabric are elegant, while standard mat board available in art supply stores offers a range of colors to enhance most any color scheme.

Many professional framers will not mat an embroidered picture unless it is going to be covered with glass. This is because few pieces are worked on fabric cut large enough to allow it to be pulled to the back and laced over hardboard. Unless a piece is fastened this way it will eventually loosen and bubble out around the mat. Assembly at home makes certain that the piece is securely fastened and thus avoids this problem.

Frames in various sizes stocked in lumber, hardware, variety, and art supply stores make it easy to find the right style for a piece that falls into standard-size ranges. Frame sections of metal or wood that snap together come in many lengths to solve some problems with irregular size, while prefinished moldings to be cut and assembled to custom measurement make it possible to frame pieces of any size. Styles run the gamut from simple narrow classics to wide, heavily carved types.

Whichever combination is chosen, it can usually be assembled at home with considerable savings. Measure mats carefully and cut with a utility knife using a new blade. Block the embroidery, and center it on a heavy chipboard cut to frame size. Pull the edges to the back and lace into place with heavy thread. (If there is not enough fabric to allow it to be pulled back, add extensions of similar weight, keeping the seams as flat as possible.)

Lacing is the best and most permanent method of fastening embroidery in a frame, and it allows for removal later for washing without damage to the fabric. Many glues will eventually discolor or rot fabric and should be avoided if possible. Chipboard is grey and sometimes imparts a dingy look to loosely woven or light-colored fabrics. To avoid this use heavy white mat board as a substitute.

A soft padded look can be achieved by placing a layer of polyester quilt batting under the embroidery and lacing it in place with a light tension. This has been done with the oval pictures on pages 78 and 102.

Place the stretched embroidery and mat (if one is to be used) in the frame. If possible, back with a cardboard and fasten with small nails or glazier's points. Glue a piece of brown wrapping paper over the entire back to seal. The paper should extend almost to the outer edges of the frame and should be glued to the frame only. When the glue has dried, dampen the paper slightly and it will shrink to the taut fit professional framers achieve.

INDEX

(Entries in **boldface** denote projects.)